Kaleidoscope

Fragments of My Life

Dustin J. Pari

DEDICATION

I hereby dedicate this book to all of you walking through this human experience with me, and I ask you to consider this:

At any given moment, you are only one decision away from an entirely different existence. Throughout this life, if you are honest with yourself, you may find that you have lived several times over. It is best to ensure all of your life's fragments are beautifully colored shards of kindness, love, and hope. Leave a legacy. Leave a rainbow. Leave a kaleidoscope.

TABLE OF CONTENTS AND ASSORTED NONSENSE

FOREWORD
BY JESSICA JEWETT

And so, we meet again. I feel like you're as much of my reader as you are Dustin Pari's reader since we've been through three books together now. Over the years, I've pushed Dustin to stretch himself more and allow people to know the real him on a deeper level. The message, I always tell him, cuts a lot deeper when it's framed inside of your own experiences. It's okay to show your humanity, your mistakes, your sorrows, and your triumphs. Anyone reading these last books can see his growth as a writer and his increasing willingness to be a three-dimensional human being rather than only a hero spreading laughter and light.

Don't get me wrong. Dustin Pari is all of these things and more. It has been my job and my privilege over the last several years to unearth the human so his example can be a shining light for other people going through similar struggles.

Near the end of my time on "our project" as he calls this book, he asked me which charity I would support if I had to choose one. It didn't take much thought on my part because I'm well-aware that I wouldn't even be here to work as Dustin's editor if it wasn't for Shriner's Hospitals. I was treated throughout my childhood at those hospitals in Salt Lake City, Utah, and St. Louis, Missouri. At least one of my nineteen surgeries was a life-saving event, which has stayed with me throughout my life. I owe Shriner's the whole of my existence. Dustin owes Shriner's for keeping me alive so we could find each other in adulthood to become professional partners and the best of friends.

You, dear reader, are holding a paperback book or a Kindle book that has made a contribution to Shriner's Hospitals' financial support. Dustin's gift to me is, in his truest form, a gift for so many children who are disabled, sick, or burn victims.

I welcome you to *Kaleidoscope*. May Dustin's inner light lead you somewhere filled with meaning, happy nonsense, and hope for the future of this little blue planet.

Jessica Jewett
March 22, 2017

Dustin J. Pari

INTRODUCTION

As a child at Monsignor Bove Elementary School in Providence, Rhode Island, I had to wear little navy blue pants and a powder blue shirt. They didn't make me wear a tie, but for a time I did anyway as I was, and still am, a fancy boy.

In kindergarten, we had a little stuffed alien named Astro. Now Astro, well, Astro was simply great. He just sat there with his empty fabric eyes and kept a watch on our class. All was well as long as we behaved, but if we acted up, things went a bit askew for ole' Astro. For you see, as a stuffed alien sent to this planet to watch five-year-old children in a Catholic school, Astro had the unique ability to take his ears off so he wouldn't have to hear us children being noisy, nor did he have to hear the kindergarten teacher take control of us rowdy rugrats. And so it went. Ears on. Ears off. Lather. Rinse. Repeat. Report to the mother ship.

As the years progressed I moved from grade to grade, while Astro and his ears remained behind in the kindergarten classroom with the tiny chairs and the little rug samples we would nap on; mine was powder blue. As I grew older life began to change. Math became more complex, studies more focused, life a little less fun, a little less magical. Astro and his memory grew smaller and smaller.

In 8th grade we started creative writing as a part of our curriculum. Finally, there was an outlet for my whimsical imagination. My mind raced with ideas and imaginative landscapes one could almost walk through as if in a dream. I wrote with great fervor. A passion burnt within me somewhere behind my bowl cut for the first time in forever.

And then it happened. My papers would come back with notes scrawled in red ink as if written by the devil himself. "Not a bad start!" "Revise!" "Punctuation!"

I was doomed. The one thing I enjoyed. The one thing I thought I was good at, stricken down with a few swipes of the teacher's pen.

There I sat, my literary crown sadly slumped down over one eye, the King of the First Draft isolated in his cold, lonely castle; the floors littered with scraps of torn up paper, shattered childhood dreams, and Astro's ears.

Now, more than 25 years later, I find myself here, aboard a flight to Minneapolis on my way to Fargo, in effort to get to a convention appearance in Mahnomen, Minnesota, where I will sell copies of my latest literary works and misadventures. To date I have co-authored two books, penned two on my own, and then there is this one here.

This book has been in my mind for many moons. Its contents have been scrawled upon pages in various notebooks piled up in my nightstand. Poems written in a soft covered journal I carried with me throughout many of my more formative years. Stories from when I was a bit more headstrong and cocksure. Files that were saved in old computers, transferred to flash drives, and revisited here. All compiled for you to read, if you should so choose to continue your journey with me.

You will find some of my earlier work a bit rough, I am sure, but give the King of The First Draft time to develop. Many of the early stories may delve into taboo subjects and be punctuated with blue humor, but to change them now would deny me of my own past. To erase the musings of that boy simply to fit the man that he has become would be to alter myself in a way that would be greatly dishonest to both you and me.

So, don't be so quick to judge or to condemn. Put that red pen in your pocket and save it for correcting your own mistakes. Lord knows I have spent a lifetime thus far correcting mine.

I hope that, as you read the pages of this book, you will see my growth, not just in my writing, but also more importantly, in my human experience. And perhaps, in some way you may even see a reflection of yourself in our shared human experience. For we all grow. We all make mistakes. We all fall. We all struggle and are made stronger. For none of us can remain a first draft forever.

I
ASSORTED MUSINGS OF A YOUNGER ME
(PARENTAL GUIDANCE IS ADVISED.)

Live from the Isle of Misfit Toys
01.11.05

With the holidays now behind us, and a new year already worn thin, it's a good time to look back and meditate on what it took to get us this far. The following is a series of semi-related, misfit thoughts.

Let us start our journey with a brief look back to just a month ago. It was a time for mistletoe and holly, and I'm not referring to the hot girl-on-girl action appearing second stage at the nudie bar's Annual Christmas Spectacular, although it was ... pretty spectacular.

I'm talking about the other holiday tradition we choose to celebrate in honor of the birth of Our Lord Jesus Christ. That's right—shopping. What better way to honor the memory of God's favorite Son than by slapping down some hard plastic and charging Chia Pets for all your friends and family? Considering the bleak economic outlook for most us middle class cogs, the season must be considered a success since the malls were packed belly buttons to buttholes. And if the icy parking lots and lack of parking spaces didn't deter you, you were then rewarded with the sight of hundreds upon hundreds of expired sperm and egg unions trying to buy a Chia Pet of their own.

As I stare around the shopping malls I cannot help but think Darwin was right in his theory of evolution, and unless we start letting some of our weak and stupid fall to the wayside, this whole planet is going to be flushed down the toilet. We are only as fast as our slowest fish.

Personally, I did my best to avoid the spawning grounds of the troubled folk, a.k.a. Walmart. But even outside of the cold clutches of Wally-world there was still plenty more simpletons, and they were infecting the holiday season like a bad case of bird flu.

Something struck me funny as I stood there in the middle of the sea of humanity's lowest common denominator, looking over at Santa Claus. Ah, jolly old Saint Nicholas! Surely he was still on the up an up. Till it dawned on me that there is a one in five chance that Santa dabbles in pedophilia and has a future as a sex offender. That's right boys and girls, it wasn't a candy cane in the old man's pocket after all. What a scam, paying money to have your child take a picture with the same wino you see on the streets the other eleven months of the year. I mean, you never see people lining up at the bar to buy a drink for some old bastard who has your kid sitting on his lap do you? But yet, here he is and so the tradition continues and somewhere strippers are helping the world a go-go around.

What about Jesus? "The reason for the season," sounds like Michael Buffer should be introducing him as he prepares to go twelve rounds for the lightweight title. Back in the day of Bethlehem, could you wait outside the stable to take your picture with the baby Jesus? That's a Polaroid I would hand over a good chunk of change for. I could see me nestled right in there between Him, Joseph, and some sheep, as a donkey lurks suspiciously in the background. I always felt for Joseph. I mean, the guy didn't even get to be with his new bride in the biblical sense and already she was pregnant with someone else's child. I still want to market t-shirts that say "Joseph: The Original Step-Dad," with his picture in the background, maybe giving some thumbs up. I really like Joseph; he's my boy.

So, what would Jesus do if he were here today? I mean, it has been quite a few years since they nailed Him to the cross and sent Him to the sky. Good little church workers everywhere are still waiting for his triumphant return even though he has yet to R.S.V.P. What if He woke up and decided today was the day? It's as good of a time as any, I suppose. War rages in the Holy Lands. People are starving all over this big rock. Suicide bombers and politicians have a good stranglehold on the fear industry. I haven't seen a Hare Krishna attempt to give me a poppy in over a decade and hardly anyone is saying, "Give peace a chance," anymore.

Most of the people are too busy cheating on everything from their taxes to their spouses to even notice what is going on around them. The rest of us are securely plugged into our iPods, which now, thank whatever deity you believe in, come equipped with the oh so necessary video playback function so that I can watch 50 Cent grind with a hood rat or gun down a thug as I wait in line to buy some apples and cake frosting at the market. Society is becoming so compartmental that soon we will not need to talk to anyone at all.

Dear Margaret,

> It's me, God.
> The machines are coming.
> Pray to them.
> > Your Friend,
> > The Big Guy

We live in a disposable society where everything is for sale and replaceable. Even in matters of redemption and salvation, it all depends on who stands up on the altar of your church in a land where chaos is running rampant and the youth is infected with this attitude of entitlement that is spreading like an incurable disease.

What if Jesus came back today? Would I even be able to get the day off work? What if He already has and no one has cared enough to take notice? All the modern-day prophets wear white jackets adorned with lots of straps and spend their days in rubber rooms, half of them thinking they are "The Great Jesu."

How do we know if one of them isn't delusional?

Remember, the only difference between prophecy and lunacy depends on what the voices in your head tell you to do.

Don't get me wrong. I'm not destined for sainthood myself, but I am hoping to at least garner an invitation to the after party upstairs. I'd like to think if I participate in many random acts of charity and kindness, they'll count for something. As a matter of fact, I'm sure St. Peter is tired of writing down how many times I selflessly break out a crisp George Washington to help some firm bottomed girl through college one song at a time.

Here's to a great New Year, ya bastards!

Note to my readers: See? I told you it was a bit rough. I think there are some good literary gems in there but you have to mine them and put them in the ol' rock polisher first. At least I think I shine more than I did when I wrote this twelve years ago. I was angry then. I saw the world decaying. I still do. But now I take steps to mend it rather than just criticize it. I spend time in church and I walk daily with God. My money goes to my family and those in need, not to the ladies on stage, but they were growing through their life experiences as well. We all have different paths. It is not for us to judge how one chooses to travel. Some of these essays I wrestled with for a long time before deciding to put them in this book, but to not include such stories would be to live a lie. None of us are perfect, but we all have room to grow, to revise.

The Final Concerto
2006

Long, long ago in a land not too far away, I met a very talented duck. I never got his name as he was busy and had no time for pleasantries, for you see, he was a working duck—the last of the Vaudevillians.

It was in the early 1980s, somewhere in New Hampshire. I was a small boy still full of hope; my dreams not yet shattered by reality; lost in a sea of bright neon colors, high hair and ripped, stone washed jeans. I was sporting a thick bowl cut and a chipper attitude. It was my family vacation after all and a small boy still full of wonder reveled in such things.

Though I'm not sure exactly what part of the Granite State we happened to be in, I do remember seeing the natural monument known as the "Man in the Mountain" and the ever popular kiddies crack heaven known as "Santa's Village".

For a nominal fee, a strapping youth waiting on descending testicles was allowed all access to Santa's workshop, which apparently was only two states away from my home the whole time. The North Pole must have been a cover for tax evasion purposes. St. Nick, you tricky son of a.... I shall hold my tongue for fear of inscription upon the naughty list.

There was a reindeer petting zoo, some straggly elves and of course the big man himself, jolly old St. Nicholas. It was magical and fantastic. Like a hand job from a woman wearing crushed velvet gloves—simply marvelous. Ah, to be young again and to believe! Could it ever be better?

Alas, like all great one night stands, even Santa's Village had to end, and that's where my aforementioned duck friend makes the scene.

On our way home from the North Pole ... err, some place in New Hampshire, my family took me to a place called "Clark's Trading Post". My memories of it are somewhat mottled, as if looking through a kaleidoscope or a stained-glass window depicting a depressing image of Jesus. (Why they never made stained glass windows of him turning water into wine or partying with His disciples, I'll never know. For some reason, they all think He wants to be remembered on that damned cross. Hear me now—when I go, don't go making mosaics of me on my deathbed, please. Especially if I die on the toilet like Elvis. Love you King!)

Nonetheless, I can still recall this Clark's Trading Post sojourn. There were many little trinkets for sale such as leather belts, bead works, greasy foods, and other various goods. I remember my family purchasing for me a black leather bracelet and some popcorn. I still love popcorn, but I'm not sure what happened to the bracelet. It might be in my bottom drawer along with other random artifacts from a childhood that lost its petals many, many moons ago.

Among the attractions at Clark's were trained animal acts, circus sideshows and the like. I want to say there was something involving a great big bear. Perhaps he danced, dove into a bucket of water, or walked a high wire while carrying a pink umbrella? Or perhaps I have watched too many cartoons and my animated memory is taking over my reality again. My apologies—the filing system in my mind is quite obsolete—I should fire the librarian if she ever steps her control-topped stocking legs out from behind the card catalog.

The bear, regardless of his marketing niche, was not my favorite attraction however, so you may disregard that colorful scrap of memory and I am sure it will be filed again, or misfiled, as the case more than likely will be, in my memory at some point soon. Anyhow, the highly-acclaimed spot of a tiny, pale-skinned, bowl haircut capped dreamer's "Favorite Attraction" was reserved for the piano playing duck that sat in his little cage in a glass box right next to the chicken who played Tic-Tac-Toe.

Personally, I always found the chicken rather pretentious. Clucking around like his chicken poop didn't stink. The duck on the other hand- well he was an entertainer! He was a fowl of substance, of style, and he was as charismatic as his bill was long.

Regardless of my loathing of the egg-headed chicken, he and my friend the duck sat there, day in and day out, in their respective pens, waiting for their show time.

Unlike the high and mighty juggling bear (he might have juggled come to think of it), the chicken and duck didn't just perform once every hour or so. These were working man's birds. They were on call from the moment the doors opened until the last customer left the tent. Kind of like doctors, but different, and not like doctors at all.

Here is how it worked: A snot-nosed kid like me would see the advertisement for the duck and chicken on the wall and beg his parents for money, tugging on the coat sleeve, asking for change. Eventually the parents would give in, and then there was a decision—chicken or duck?

As soon as your money was in, the red light in the cage flipped on and the magic started. The chicken approached the glass and made his selection on the other side of the Tic-Tac-Toe board. Then you made your choice. Red X's or O's popped up in their respective places. And eventually you or the chicken would win (and yes, the chicken did win from time to time). Regardless of the outcome, the chicken got his little treat from the dispenser and sat back on his high horse, or nest, as the case would be.

My boy the duck was a fowl of a different feather. When his light came on, it was show time, baby! And boy was he something. I bet if he could have gotten out of that cage and back in the barnyard, he could have had any little honey he wanted. He was a flat-footed Casanova. A duck billed Don Juan. What girl could resist his charming advances?

The moment that bulb flickered to life, he waddled his little feathered bottom over to his tiny piano in the corner, stretched out his neck and hammered out a tune with his bill. Simply brilliant! Bravo, my good friend! Any fool can play Tic-Tac-Toe but you, my boy, are a maestro! A master of the arts! A tickler of the ivories! Take a bow and enjoy your little duck pellet, my good man, for it is well deserved.

In reality it was just a simple tune but fitting since he was a simple duck; and together it was more than any six-year-old boy, staring wide eyed from beneath his bowl cut, could dream of while living in a simple world, which time proved is the best kind of world after all. It's no coincidence that the first instrument I ever played was a small electric organ. Although I never achieved the same public acclaim as that beautiful little duck, it made me happy.

Now I sit here, many, many years later, long past the family road trips that dotted the highway of my youth. My little piano playing duck is long since dead, along with my innocence. They are both buried in the dust and rubble of memories and experiences that have compiled during many sunrises and sunsets.

For now, there is no magic left in this old silk hat. The show is over. It's a shame that when people start explaining the mysteries of childhood, the mysteries of life, part of you starts dying.

The death of Santa Claus is your own.

I found myself awake the other night thinking of that duck. I haven't seriously thought of him since I left New Hampshire that summer. It's strange how your mind works sometimes. Strange not to think of something for so long and then to remember it so fondly as if I could still feel the cool glass pressed against my flesh, as if I could still hear the tiny notes squeaking from his piano. The tap, tap, tapping of his bill on the keys, the soft glow of the light reflecting off the glass. I can almost taste the popcorn.

Yet, here I am. A 28-year-old boy who misses his musical duck; a friend who was long since neglected and forgotten; a boy who misses his childhood and his dreams, such wonderful dreams. I wonder what his last days were like. I wonder if they ever let him out of that cage to stretch his wings and mingle with his groupies. Did he resent the chicken as much as I did? All I can do is imagine his twilight years and that faded red light coming on, signaling the start of what would be his last performance.

He gets up, arthritic little orange legs threatening to give out under his frail frame with each wobbly step. He waddles over toward his tiny Baby Grand, a little slower than before, for one last performance. Yes, this will be his masterpiece, his Mona Lisa, his Persistence of Time. He will play once more. Just once more. The notes are tiny and quiet, yet beautiful and sweet. His bill moves slowly with measured steps, hitting his notes perfectly every time. His head grows heavy and his vision blurs. Oh death, carry me over for another year!

He plays his final note and his tiny bill does not rise over the keys again. The show is over—he is finally free.

The Boston Story
July 2007

Today I had to go take the Homeland Security test at the JFK building in Boston since they were hiring INS officers to assist in enforcing immigration laws.

I felt like such a "Big Boy" on the train; and no, I don't mean the popular southern restaurant chain.

Seriously, I am thirty-years-old and still cannot travel to Boston without first consulting with my good friend, Jeff Ouimette, who works up in the city about my train selection. Perhaps I should not be applying for a job when I must study just to make the trip.

I was all set for my big day. I had my little black leather portfolio, which to the other travelers may have made me look like a serious man about town, although inside it merely contained my directions for which trains to take and when to take them, some oatmeal granola bars, and a Snapple bottle cap that read: "True Fact: Ducks cannot walk without bobbing their heads."

Yup, nothing says, "I am ready for a serious career," like snacks and foolishness.

The bottle cap must have distracted me when the train came to a stop as I got off at the wrong place. I had to wait for the next train to come by, only to then get confused at the Red Line, and thus I was forced to rely on the friendly and informative employees of the MBTA. Whom, when I asked where to pay for the subway, merely shoved a card in my hand and yelled, "ADD VALUE!" in a horrible comedian Wanda Sykes type voice. As if Wanda Sykes' voice isn't bad enough.

I tried to give the Wanda Sykes-like MBTA lady some money to "add value," but she angrily pointed me to a machine. I tried sticking my card in the slot, since in most instances in life I have done this same maneuver with reasonable success, but alas this was not the case here in Beantown. Instead I had the same cantankerous Sykes wannabe yelling, "ADD VALUE!" over my shoulder again. Son ... of ... a ... bitch.

Finally, I added value and was on the Red Line, just moments away from taking a step that could lead me to a new career— hopefully one that would support my family and give me some sort of pension when all is said and done. Finally, a real job with retirement possibilities, one that I would even have to commute to. In my mind, I could see myself reading the paper on the train every morning and striking up friendly banter with the conductor and ticket takers. Maybe we would even sing a song of sorts; my great musical morning. Somewhere in the back of my head that old familiar song was playing; "My baby takes the morning train, he works from nine to five and then...." Ah yes, look out illegal immigrants! There's a new sheriff in town. Dustin Pari is the name, enforcing immigration laws is my game!

To be honest, I'm not sure what exactly my duties would entail as an INS officer but I picture myself like Crockett in *Miami Vice*, busting into places, badge held high, while illegals scamper for the back-door yelling, "Immigration! I-N-S! I-N-S!" Maybe the government would even assign me to an ethnically diverse partner I could lovingly call Tubbs; barring he wasn't overweight and sensitive.

I had finally arrived at Government Center when my buddy Jeff called to check on me. It was two minutes to test time so I couldn't talk as I had to go through security and all that jazz. But it was nice of him to make sure I arrived safely and didn't end up being raped in some dark forgotten corner in the smoky gullet of the subway. I received a text from my wife telling me she loved me and wishing me luck on the exam, which was very nice since everything I do is for her and our family.

The test was easy. I would honestly be surprised if I had gotten more than four or five answers incorrect, if that. It had three parts. The first was a simple task of identifying which phrase was supported by the above paragraph. The second was English grammar and spelling. I was almost tripped up on occasion and felt rather foolish after being so cocksure earlier on. But luckily, I was able to pull it back together with enough time to doodle on my Government Issued scrap paper. (I kid you not. They give you their own "Government Issued" scrap paper.)

The third part was a personality survey and standard psych evaluation. One question stood out to me. What would your co-workers say about you? I put down that they would say that I was the best at everything. Every question like that which asked about my abilities, I gave myself the highest accolades possible. Let them hire me if they want to prove me wrong.

I also wouldn't answer the question as to what my greatest

weakness is. If I have learned one thing from comic books, it's that you should never let anyone know your weakness because it'll only come back to bite you in your hindquarters.

I had also finished this third section with plenty of time and commenced to doodle on my government issued scrap paper whilst the woman next to me was dutifully and meticulously checking her answers on the personality section. I thought perhaps she had multiple personalities and one was merely checking up on the other.

Finally, the test was over and they collected the test booklets and answer keys. I started plotting my course home and was about to throw out my scrap paper when the proctor asked us to please hand them in. That's right. Please hand in your scrap paper. Hmm?

I didn't know what to say. I looked around and here were people with various notes and spellings of test words on their papers; and then there was mine that consisted of a caveman like sketch of a talking dog with a dialogue bubble that said, "Ducks cannot walk without bobbing their heads," repeatedly.

The scrap paper was probably the real test, and now the government will not only dismiss my application but they will probably put me on the No-Fly list or something like that. I hope Tubbs at least gets a good partner; someone better than me. Someone he deserves.

As for me, it's just another day in the ongoing misadventure that is my life. I think I'll sing "The Trolley Song" Judy Garland style as I ride home with my little black leather portfolio and bottle cap.

Note to my readers: Needless to say, the government never called me about the position. However, the trip was not without its own rewards. I learned that commuting up to Boston isn't really like a musical, and thus, not for me. I also cannot look at ducks without thinking of the lesson learned from the simple Snapple bottle cap. As it pertains to immigration, I'm all for people working to change their stars but feel it should be done in a legal manner.

Jingle Brains
11.05.07

They say one of the greatest accidental inventions was penicillin; and up till today, that may have very well been true.

I'm experiencing a little bit of a head cold and have been sick for the past few days. The usual symptoms: stuffiness, fever, dark urination, and the overwhelming urge to eat Chinese food while watching *Weekend at Bernie's 2*. (That's right, not even the original *Weekend at Bernie's* in which you suspended disbelief for a bit, but the sequel that is even more preposterous, if you can believe that.)

There I sat with the Kleenex box at my hip as if I were the Billy the Kid of cold fighting and the showdown with mucus was fast approaching. It was still a few minutes before high noon, and since that's when all notable battles begin, I had a few minutes to kill. I decided to treat myself to a large glass of eggnog. 'Tis the season after all. They have many new varieties this year—one of which I'm partial to and strongly recommend. Sugar cookie flavored eggnog. Sweet Christmas, that stuff is good! Like getting a hand job from a woman wearing velvet gloves.

Regardless of my penchant for sugar cookie flavoring or flights of fancy with ladies in velvet gloves, this particular glass of nog was the classic variety that has brought joy to the hearts of millions of poor slobs like myself every year around the holiday season. *Mm-mm!* So thick and creamy that it sticks to the glass after you repeatedly try to rinse it out. Like getting poop on your shoe, but in a good way. There really is nothing else like it. It doesn't taste at all like eggs, thankfully—and since there is no other type of nog available, the title of this heavenly beverage could simply be "Nog—as if angels put all the wonderful flavors of Heaven in a blender so ye mere mortals may sample a taste of the good life at least once a year." Of course, that tile would be a bitch for marketing purposes and the label on the carton would be bloody ridiculous, so perhaps somehow simple eggnog is best after all. I must learn not to question simple things.

As I raised my glass to drink this heavenly nectar, it teased at my lips and softly wrapped itself around my tongue like the kiss of a lovely gypsy girl at harvest time. Slowly coating my throat and sliding deep into my belly where it would sit and nourish the spark of joy and hope that I still cling to in this troubled world of thieves and heroes.

Ah, yes…. Eggnog.

How I'd like to buy the world some nog and teach them to sing in perfect harmony; or at least not be such jerks to each other. Seriously people, we are all in it together. Whether you see this for yourself now or later when the deity of your choosing points it out in the video review of your life, you will eventually see it as truth.

Betwixt these musings and meanderings of a kind-hearted boy in love with his beverage, there suddenly arose such a clatter in my sinus cavity that my hand shot to the tissue box to take care of the matter. It was high noon and here I was caught daydreaming about eggnog, idiot that I am. I would have never survived in the Wild West.

A quick honk and a toot and then … what's this? What type of magic is happening? Suddenly my head is filled with Christmas! There must have been some magic in that old eggnog I found, for after blowing my nose my brain began to dance around. The taste of eggnog amplified through my skull like a pirate ship full of merry elves singing Yuletide carols to a steady drum beat, as well wishes for mankind played in my tattered mind and oozed up behind my red and green ornament eyes.

Never in my life have I had such an experience.

A simple quick swig of eggnog followed by the blowing of one's nose fills the sinus cavity with euphoric sensations and good will toward men.

Behold, for unto you a child has been born this day!

Merry Christmas to all!

May the body and blood of Christ bring us all to everlasting life, or may the deity of your choosing bless you accordingly. Either way, let us live in peace and harmony, and share a glass of eggnog.

Note to my readers: Do try this eggnog exercise. It is pure magic.

You Say You Want A Revolution
05.18.08

All you need is love according to The Beatles, and who am I ever to question the Prophets John, Paul, George, and Ringo? More than forty years has passed since the four lads from Liverpool left the Cavern Club and invaded the Ed Sullivan show, and now everything is a complete mess. If there was ever a time in which the world needed a mop-topped hero, now is it. I must face the facts; half of my heroes are dead and the forecast for tomorrow is gloomy at best.

Every time I fill up my little pickup truck, I'm amazed at the number that magically appears when the last drop of sweet crude travels down the thirsty neck of my rusty gas tank like a wayward sperm that chose the wrong fallopian tube. There appears to be no rhyme or reason to the pricing and it simply climbs higher and higher each time I need a little more go-go juice. Like a magic eight ball that never gives an optimistic response, I stare at the digital pump display in hopes that somehow through the murky purple depths will arise a favorable amount. The most I ever seem to get is "try again later." It's getting to the point where a weekly paycheck just about pays for the commute to and from work.

Where is the reward in that?

The nightly news is filled with the same reports of government plans that never seem to work. Stories of an endless war that has raged on for so long most don't even report on it anymore. Children from across the country are still being shipped off to fight mystery opponents which appear to change with the daily accepted definition of who is and who is not a terrorist.

And things are not much better on the home front.

Full-time employed college graduates can be seen visiting local food shelters in search of discounted beans in which to provide sustenance for themselves and their families. Home foreclosures are at a record high and climbing, as many families do not know where next month's mortgage payment is coming from. How long can they hold out? Bees aren't making honey like they used to and scientists are baffled. It's true. Just Google it.

Is there an end in sight to any of these problems? I certainly don't have any answers. I do have some questions.

Where are the radicals?

Where are the flower power children of this generation?

Where are the demonstrations?

The sit-ins?

Where are Rosa Parks and Wavy Gravy when you need them?

Has the government finally used enough scare tactics so that there is not even a threat of revolution?

Or have we all been distracted enough with clever reality television shows and handheld electronics that we simply don't have the time to rage against the machine anymore?

"No iPhone! No Peace!" Now there's a slogan we can get behind. For now, I am but a lone voice crying out in the dark for change. I hope to stir change even if it's just a little bit. I hope to organize and fight just as soon as we can all find a date and time where we won't be missing any of our favorite shows. Sigh. This revolution will not be televised, though TiVo may sponsor it, and in any case, it can always be downloaded as a podcast for your viewing convenience.

Christmas At Vicky's
12.03.08

With the Christmas season upon me, I ventured into the snowy masses, despite my better judgment, to the mall. My intentions were noble; to buy a few gifts for my close friends, family, and that special lady in my life that I call Wife. As with all best laid plans, things eventually went staggering askew like the town drunk after happy hour.

It started as I passed the Victoria Secret and noticed the mannequin in the window with her naughty little Santa hat and a very suggestive red and white-laced outfit. It probably started long before that, like when I was seven or eight-years-old and I saw those large 1980s Christmas lights that people would use on the shrubbery in their front yards. For some reason I got that special feeling down in my Oshkosh overalls but for the sake of this moment, we'll blame it on the saucy mannequin.

My head became filled with visions of hot holiday erotic misadventures all trimmed in Christmas lights and candy canes. My sweet, sugar induced, electric sex fantasy. This year Santa was going to bring me what I wanted whether his jolly fat ass wanted to slide it down my chimney or not. I was going to take it into my own hands. What the hell? I had been a good boy after all.

With a full wallet and that special tingly feeling downstairs, I journeyed into the lace and silk filled fantasyland that gives so many a young man that nervous feeling in his stomach. With just a quick glance around I knew that this was going to be a Christmas to remember, like the ones old crooners from the 1940s used to sing about. I'm dreaming of a silky white teddy Christmas just like the ones I used to know.

I perused the thongs, dabbled in the teddies, and settled my eyes upon a nice sexy yet conservative outfit. I like my lady to feel attractive but not trashy. I prefer old school sensuality to the tawdriness of today's little harlots. It was a red satiny number with just a bit of white fluffy stuff across the bosom. Ah, the bosom! What better pillow for one to rest his head upon and dream?

Now, as a man, it is difficult to grasp the sizing of ladies' unmentionables, but I consider myself a man willing to expand his horizons and put in a valiant effort when it comes to things I do not fully understand. Although by this age I think I should have a better grasp of it than I do. I think the problem lies within the difference between the sexes. A man underwear comes in about three different styles and four sizes. You have the breezy boxers, the athletic boxer/underwear combo, and the classic tighty-whities. I myself enjoy the freedom of the boxer shorts because they allow certain liberations for my good friend with the one squinty eye in the downstairs apartment. He does enjoy a healthy stretch in the morning when he gets out of bed; but don't we all?

With the sophisticated garments of the woman there are a great many choices. The varieties I saw included: the thong, the G-string, the V-string, the bikini-cut, the boy shorts, the granny panty, the push-up bra, the water bra, the under wire, the no wire, the crisscross, and many more. Then there were other even more bewildering options like seamless, strapless, and crotch-less, for the lady on the move.

One option that has always led me to much humiliation is the front clasping bra. I cannot tell you how many hot nights I have been fumbling around frustrated in the dark searching the desert of a woman's back for that damned elusive clasp only to find out that it was up front. What an idiot.

Even when I know it is in the front I am useless. I get so distracted by the beautiful valley betwixt which the clasp is nestled that I cannot focus enough to get it undone. Trying to unclasp that thing is like trying to tie your shoes with mittens on! All the time the girl is staring at you, judging you, weighing your abilities, and you are coming up as one whom is unworthy to have a balcony view.

Back at the store I find myself with the overwhelming guilty feeling of a little boy staying up late to peer in on his older sister's pajama party. A bead of sweat starts to emerge on my brow as I inexplicably fumble through the drawers to find the right size. Oh, why do they have to be in drawers! Is it not awkward enough for a man to be in a fancy woman's lingerie store? Must they make you feel like pervert on a college panty raid? Hang those damn things up on tiny satin hangars!

And just when you think it can't possibly get any worse, over walks the ridiculously attractive sales girl. I freeze like a convict in the searchlight after jumping over the prison wall. I can hear the search dogs barking somewhere in the back of my animated mind; the air raid siren wailing.

"Can I help you, sir?"

Suddenly I am back at my seventh grade dance with sweaty palms and about as much courage as the cowardly lion prior to seeing the wizard.

Here I stand a trembling, bumbling idiot in the middle of a crowded sex shop confronted by a beautiful woman. I feel like I have been going through her panty drawer and now she caught me with my hand in the cookie jar. D'oh!

I mumbled what I was looking for, the numbers of the sizes racing through my head like some strange algebra equation. Let's see … now it was 36C x Small = the square of something…. Yeah, that's her size.

The sales girl sensing I'm an idiot tries to make it simpler for me, her Neanderthal customer who just wants to live out a little triple X-Mas fantasy.

"Is she about my size?" she asks while holding it up against her curvaceous body.

Great. Now all I had was the mental image of her in that outfit. I became quite flustered and a bit hot under the collar. I might as well go home and boil myself in my own pudding, if you catch my snowdrift.

Christmas…. Bah Humbug!

Note to my readers: Ummm… well, some things never change.

Magic Feathers
01.22.09

The more I look around this world, the more I see people slipping off the path, sliding into depression, and giving up hope. I just wanted to offer up this little theory of mine as something to think about, and perhaps you can think about it and maybe you can even relate to it or you know someone who can relate to it and you can help him or her.

It seems in today's busy world, there is little or no time for encouragement of others. I have worked countless jobs where I have seen good employees, stray off the path and falter, and all they really needed was a little sign of confidence in them from the boss. Personally, I hate the word boss as there is only one person I answer to. He rules over everything and He told us all to call him Father. He's not big on titles. No one with true power ever really is. It is love and respect that counts, not empty titles.

It just seems that in today's compartmentalized society where people are plugged into their iPods, playing games on their iPhones, or busy uploading their own videos to YouTube to glean their fifteen megabytes of fame, we are all too preoccupied to take notice of those around us and interact. This leaves a lot of people feeling disconnected from each other, and thus we are slipping further and further off the path.

Perhaps you have seen the studies done with those cute little baby monkeys and their "moms". The scientists put two baby monkeys in separate areas, one with a real mother who can fully interact with and embrace the child, the other baby monkey has a fake dummy mother who provides nothing more than food. Obviously, the nurtured little monkey grows up in a better situation and, when is given the chance to interact with others, has an easier time adapting. The other monkey, not so much.

In many ways, we are becoming a society of sad little monkeys. We grow up without anyone to tell us they are proud of us, that we are doing a good job, or that they believe in us. And then we carry that burden further into our adolescent and adult lives.

I see people struggling everywhere; in line at the store, at work, and in all aspects of my day-to-day life. Wouldn't it be nice if we noticed someone like that in our own lives and just tried to show them that someone still believes in them? Just help to nurture that spark of life that will someday propel them to greater things? It doesn't cost a damn thing to do, and it can yield a world of good!

I often hearken back to the Disney classic movie *Dumbo*, which I am sure they have locked in the Disney Vault so people will scamper to buy it next time it becomes available. Good ol' Disney; a happy mouse smiling from the bow of the ship, and a marketing devil at the wheel. I love the company, but boy do they know how to make it easy for you to give them money. Well-played, Mouse. Well played.

In *Dumbo*, you will no doubt remember that, as in most early Disney films, our loveable little hero is separated from his mother. At least Dumbo's mom only gets locked up in isolation for getting mad and she doesn't get shot in the opening scene like poor Bambi's mother. Seriously, who thought these were great things to show children?

With the departure of the family matriarch, enters Dumbo's one and only friend, Timothy Q. Mouse. (I have no idea what the "Q" stands for. I am sure you can Google it. Me? I like some mystery in life.) But tiny Tim believes in him. He gives Dumbo courage, strength and hope. He gives him the idea of a better future and a brighter tomorrow. He gives him the slightest hope that all is not lost, that he has not been abandoned. He gives him, a magic feather. Of course, the feather is not really magic, but for once, Dumbo believes in something. He thinks it's a feather that is his savior, but it's really himself.

It is my own personal theory that we can be like Timothy Q. Mouse and search out those people in our lives who just need a little bit of encouragement. People who just need someone to tell him or her they are doing a good job, someone to believe in them. It's also important to make sure they do not grow too dependent. At some point, Timmy Q. had to pull the feather out from under his friend and show him that he didn't need it after all, but that he could soar on his own.

I encourage anyone who reads this to try and be positive to those around you, to unplug from our own little world, and be aware of those who walk the road alongside us. They may need a little help. They may need a little lift. They may need you, for a time, to be their magic feather.

Note to my readers: I love Disney. I enjoy taking my family there for vacation. I enjoy their products. I have even taken a Disney Management course. I really like the backstory of how it all came to be, and how it continues to grow. But it is important to note that it was not an overnight success. Neither are we. Dumbo wasn't quite ready to fly right away. Give yourself reasonable time to grow, to soar.

The Mattress and the Messiah
April of 2009

I'm never sure what it is about April but it's just one of those things that has no explanation, I suppose. Like why hot dogs come in packs of eight and hot dog rolls come in packs of ten. Or why I get so ridiculously happy when my iPod plays a double shot of my favorite artist. Whether it is cosmic, coincidental, or simply curious, there are things in this life that are beyond our understanding. And, starting off April in a period of emotional turbulence is something that is very commonplace for me. But, it never lasts long and as the years have progressed it seems to be briefer each time. Maybe next year April will be perfect.

Anyhow, while in a period of quiet contemplation, meditation and prayer these last few days, I started viewing the human struggle in a more refined way.

It is incredibly human to stumble from time to time. To fall and to rise again; swelling like the majestic waves of the ocean, a transition from chaotic turbulence to serene solitude. It's a seemingly endless cycle—almost to the point of insanity. However, for those with enough fortitude and pure grit to stick it out to the end, it is incredibly rewarding.

Being a fellow of certain religious and spiritual convictions, I could not help but to notice the coincidence of my own phoenix patterns in relation to the timing of the Easter season in the liturgical year. And if it was okay for Jesus to fall a few times before the ultimate sacrifice and redemption, then it is more than acceptable for me to stumble and to have some trying times while traveling this road. I think that's something important for all of us to keep in mind as we walk together in life. The times when we fall short of our own expectations, the times we fail, the beatings we endure; none of it really matters if you keep getting back up. That's what counts. The struggles that we encounter on our way to the goal only help to build character and make for that much more enjoyable a victory dance.

I recalled my friend Darren Valedofsky telling me during a conversation we had while he was driving home from work one night that he saw a homeless man sleeping on the cold sidewalk, while only a few blocks beyond him was a discarded mattress lying empty along the roadside. The man was two blocks from a slightly better situation, if only he could have continued. It may not have changed his life but perhaps it may have offered him just a touch more comfort, leaving him stronger for tomorrow's journey and whatever was ahead of him.

Persistence, perseverance, and pure belief in oneself, and the Lord, can go a long way. And when those times come along that get in our heads, that make us feel broken, beaten, and scarred, I think it's important to remember that story of the homeless man and the mattress; for we may not know what is just ahead of us, but we will never know- if we simply do not continue.

Note to my readers: This story really resonated with me. It became a turning point in my life, and thus I still use it today in many of my motivational lectures. I urge you all to never give up, no matter how hard or dark things may become, for you have no idea what is waiting just beyond the horizon.

The Reality of Reality TV
04.14.09

You sit there below a little cardboard sign with your name on it. A thin blue curtain separates you from your own childhood television heroes that are sitting behind you, on their side of the curtain, underneath a similar little cardboard sign with their name on it. This is the convention circuit. The ComiCons.

You sit behind a 6-foot wooden table draped in a simple white cloth, imprisoned behind a stack of photos that you carried here yourself. A stack of photos that you had printed at Staples, packaged in a big box, and carried through airport security. You tell them it's just a box of pictures. The TSA agent persists with their questioning and you regrettably confess they are pictures of you, and you feel like a complete and utter moron. A twisted, little egomaniac. You want to tell them the whole story. You want to tell them that you aren't a self-absorbed individual with a distorted view of himself. You want to tell them this, but you don't. You take off your shoes and show them your little bag of eye drops and hand lotion, which they probably think you are going to use in the airplane bathroom in an effort to join the mile-high club by yourself, or worse, maybe with your collection of paper self-portraits.

Inevitably your flight lands and you are off to the next show, the next convention, the next promotional appearance, and the next event. Back behind the wooden table with a white cloth that is just better than the one at your high school prom but not as nice as the one at your wedding. You miss your wife. You miss your daughter. But you smile nonetheless and sign your name. And sign your name. And sign your name.

You take a photo with your arm around another stranger, and you sign your name, and you sign your name, and you sign your name. You never let your fans see the human inside the hero. Never let them see the man behind the curtain. Cover the stab marks in your back with your cape. Chin up. Eyes focused. "Smile!" Flash. "Smile!" Flash. And you sign your name. And you sign your name. And you sign your name.

You put the little cap back on the Sharpie. You stand and you wait. You take a picture. You sign your name. You wonder how you got here. You sign your name. You wonder how your childhood hero feels on the other side of the curtain. You sign your name.

Someone asks you what it's like to be a celebrity. You want to tell them the truth. You want to tell them that if anyone ever gives them the choice between fame and fortune, choose fortune. Don't be an idiot. Take the money and run. Popularity is useful only in high school. It may help you to get the head cheerleader's panties to decorate the floor of your bedroom, but in the real world, you need money.

You want to tell them that being a D List "celebrity" is far from as glamorous as they think it is. You want to tell them about how tight your personal budget is. How you must leave more than three quarters of your per diem check at home just to pay some bills. You want to tell them about how you've been eating peanut butter and Nutella sandwiches almost exclusively for over two and a half weeks because it's the only thing you can afford when you were filming at glorious locations on the other side of the globe. You want to tell them about doing laundry in the hotel sink, again and again and again, your socks never fully drying. You want to tell them this but you don't. You smile, and you sign your name.

You want to tell them the story about the night your wife called saying that your daughter may have had a seizure and how the ambulance had to come to your house. How you were worried because only you knew that the health care hadn't been paid. About how you cried in your hotel room, feeling helpless; feeling like a bad father, feeling like a bad husband knowing that you took this position to try and better their situation through your own sacrifice and instead it appears you have made it worse. Once again, the family cow was traded for a handful of dreams, for the hopes of a brighter tomorrow. But you don't say anything. You smile. You give them a hug. You sign your name.

They ask you about certain episodes hoping for a behind the scenes story of life changing revelation. They ask if you ever thought you would be famous. They want to know how were you discovered. And you want to tell them about dealing with production companies and agents; about how contract negotiations operate on threats, lies, and by fear mongering.

Don't ask for this or you will lose your position.

Be happy with what you have or you will be fired.

Don't threaten to quit or you will be sued for every dollar you ever made and then some.

These people behind the camera behind the camera, who take credit for making you who you are, when in truth these people are no one themselves. Just boogeymen. Dark shadows that are vacant, cold, and unfeeling behind their plastic smiling masks and sleazy handshakes.

Someone asks you to give advice to his or her kids about the business. Record a voice mail for them. You are their favorite cast member. You are an inspiration. You tell them to aim higher, and to do better. They laugh not knowing how serious you are. So you smile, and you sign your name.

You want to tell them that your agent has his hands tied because the production company threatened him with litigation if he even tried to contact them. You want to tell them that you never have even met the person who runs the company you work for. The guy who signs your paychecks is only memorable as a threatening voice on your cell phone messaging system; a small man behind a big curtain; an anonymous monster. You have never even spoke to him yourself, but he sounds like a complete and total clown.

A woman asks how much your photos are. You tell her twenty bucks, but you want to tell her that you would give them away for free if only you were paid enough to cover your own health insurance. You want to tell her that you tried to get just a bit more, not because you think you are a big celebrity, but because you need to provide for your family. But the company said no, and your agent is still taking his commission. They threatened to replace you instead of giving you more money. So it's twenty bucks, sorry. I truly, truly am. You have no idea how sorry I am.

You go back to your hotel room alone. You pack your suitcase and go to the airport in the morning, alone. You eat a six dollar slice of pizza and drink an eight dollar beer alone at the bar in Terminal B. You board your first flight. You board your second flight. You get in your rental car and drive a few hours down the highway alone. You find your way to the hotel. Wash up. Shower. Shave. Go to the event floor and find your next little table with the thin white tablecloth as it sits there vacant beneath the cardboard sign with your name. Strangely this sight echoes how you feel inside; hollow and alone. You put out your stack of photos. You smile. You sign your name.

You want to tell these good people who are giving you their hard-earned cash that it shouldn't have to be this way. That the faceless voice on your cell phone message—that he has a private jet. That he flies back and forth from LA to Vegas to watch Ultimate Fighting. To watch men beat themselves to a bloody pulp. As he sits there, in a modern-day coliseum. Feeling like a self-righteous emperor, sipping single malt scotch while the gladiators battle below. How he is basically just indulging in a sheltered homoerotic fantasy that he doesn't have the balls to admit. Not that there's anything wrong with it. The only real sin is being afraid to be who you truly are.

These limousine riding and jet flying mystery men, they are full of nonsense.

They tell your agent to go perform unspeakable acts upon his own mother.

They call him a pariah. They make it clear they don't care about you, his client.

That night you were up crying, worried sick about your child. They didn't so much as send an email asking how she was, how you were doing. They definitely didn't call saying they would give you enough money so you could afford healthcare.

They had a lawyer call your agent. Telling him that money within the company was tight. That despite the great ratings, the show barely got picked up. That at this point it's not a profitable venture. That you aren't getting anything extra so stop asking or it's a lawsuit.

These Hollywood big shots whose fancy suits have more moral fiber than they do.

These guys with egos twenty times bigger than their manhood. These would be the people to be killed first in a post-apocalyptic world. They would be paralyzed with fear. Crying, clutching their cell phones, staring at their overpriced bullshit watches, wondering how much time they had left. Tick. Tick. Tick.

These are the people currently pulling the strings. Forcing you to dance, week in and week out in front of millions of viewers worldwide while they go home to their families, their mistresses, their Ultimate Fighting event with their private jet.

But the show is not profitable.

It barely got picked up.

You, there in the bathroom, ringing your socks out and hanging them in the shower to dry. You, going to bed in a lonely hotel room again.

You, on the other side of the world, far away from your family. You aren't worth anything more.

All of this, playing out in your head while you are a featured guest at this event or that event, beneath that little cardboard sign with your name on it. All of this eating at your heart, at your pride, all of this, behind that stack of 8x10s with your picture on it. Smiling. Signing your name. The show must go on.

You do it for your family. You do it for the people who look up to you. You keep on doing it because you don't want to admit defeat. Inside you're dying but you'll be damned if you tap out to these self-righteous ass-clowns in oversized designer floppy shoes.

Behind that glimmering white smile and rock star appearance is a guy who cries in his hotel room. Behind that perfect hair forever is a simple man who is just doing the best he can. But the bull is dying.

He is dealing with the same struggles, just like everyone else watching him along at home.

A simple man on a very, very slightly elevated platform, just trying to keep it all together for the ones he loves, even though it appears the deck is stacked against him. He is grateful, thankful, and he will not give up.

You sign your name. You sign your name. You sign your name.

You smile and speak positively for the fans. You do truly care for them after all. None of this is their fault. They don't know the reality of your reality. You take a picture. You put the cap back on the black Sharpie once again. You stand and wait for the next person to come and ask how much your pictures are, hoping that you'll make enough to cover the mortgage this month, wondering when you will see home again.

And just like your own childhood hero, secluded behind their own headshots, just on the other side of the thin blue curtain, you know inside... the show must go on.

Note to my readers: This may be the one story I wrestled with the most. All of it is true. All of it. I wish it wasn't, but at the same time, I am so thankful for the opportunities that have been placed before me, I never want to complain about them and I never have.

This essay, done many moons ago when I decided I was going to leave the *Ghost Hunters International* show, is the only written account of my struggles, and it barely scratches the surface. However, I am someone who looks for that silver lining and when the clouds are simply too gray, well, I just enjoy the rain. And so, I did what I had to do as a father and a husband. I do what I still do today. I go forward. I work. I find a way to provide, no matter what.

I know to some it may not seem like a hard gig, and I know there are far worst things one must do to make a living than travel and sign their name, but when you do all of this on top of a regular 9-5 that is more like an 8-6, it gets tiring, lonely, and frustrating. It also does not come about easily. Many miles and sleepless nights had to be logged and lived to get my name on that little cardboard sign.

The people, the faces, and the places that I have seen on this journey are amazing. I have acquaintances all over the world and some good friends scattered like diamonds in between. I have a special place in my heart for so many of you that you may never know. Those smiles in the pictures, they are sincere, even if I am more of a grinner than a big smiling fellow. That warmth you feel in my hug, that is real. The fact that you want me to sign my photo for you still amazes me. But life on the road has never been easy.

Strangely, all of this … it has been the only life I have known for so long that I have somehow come to embrace it. I wouldn't say that I am in love with it, but I understand it. I respect it. I've danced with it throughout time. I know how to make it work. I know when to book the cheapest flights. I know my way around airports, late night gas stations, and empty highways that stretch out beneath starless skies when all the people I love are far away and sleeping.

Many things have been said about me, both good and bad. Listen to whom you want and believe what you will. Out of all the things I have heard, I think I appreciate the following the most: That I am kind, and that I have an incredible work ethic. Those things mean a lot to me. I do all I can for all I can. I am exhausted most of the time, sure. But I honestly believe that all of this has merely been precursor for what's next. I know in my heart, in the cavern of my soul, deep down in a place that only God knows, that my best is still yet to come. I encourage you to stay tuned.

Vaguely Interesting Things About Me
or
My Intimate Dance with Peculiarity and Flights of Fancy
05.27.09

Of all my senses, hearing is the only one that really works. Without my contacts, I can't see past my arm's length. This probably came from a childhood game I invented called "Spin Around Until You're Dizzy and Then Lie Down and Stare Directly At the Sun". I think you can gather from the title what the game entailed.

My sinuses have always been screwed and thus my nose is for decorative purposes only as I do enjoy wearing fancy sunglasses and something needs to hold them up.

My sense of touch is pretty much okay too but I'm just not a touchy-feely person, so I probably use it the least. Seriously, outside of sex, kissing, holding hands, and making sure you don't burn or freeze your naughty parts in the shower, how much is there to touch? Okay, probably a lot. But I digress and I digest. I suppose I like touching. Textures turn me on.

Hearing, however, has never failed me. Sometimes my wife thinks I don't hear things that she says, but in my defense, I truly get distracted easily and it's tough to keep my train of thought from derailing. I may have Attention Deficit Disorder but I don't sit still long enough for them to test me.

I moo at cows. Anytime I see them on the roadsides I must at least beep the horn, and if possible, roll down the window and give them a heartfelt moo. It's a sign of kinship upon this earth. We are in it together. They are just slower and delicious next to a baked potato adorned with butter and bits of pig. Pigs say oink.

Music is the best way for me to remember things. I honestly could not tell you which pair of boxers I put on this morning or what I ate last night for dinner, but I can tell you that the first time I heard Bobby McFerrin sing "Don't Worry, Be Happy". I was in my mom's silver 1984 Camry on my way home from elementary school.

Throughout school I needed more than a mere pneumonic to remember answers to testing material. The only real regurgitate and repeat bits of history and biology that I can still recite are all linked to some song I made up, or in the very least, a dirty limerick.

I have never truly felt comfortable around girls who wear a lot of makeup.

Those really large, nineteen eighties-esque Christmas lights that people use to decorate their front lawn shrubbery make me horny. I have no logical explanation or extended reasoning for it. It's just one of those things. Also on the list of things that get me primed for intercourse are the smell of fresh paint and the first gentle breezes of springtime. Combine them and I am like a powder keg in an old Yosemite Sam cartoon. Ka-boom baby!

I lose things quite a bit. This probably ties in with the fact that I am easily distracted and more than likely has nothing to do with cows, Christmas lights, paint fumes, or anything else. One of the first places I always check for lost objects is the refrigerator. So far it has yet to turn up any of the missing items in question but it seems like a viable location full of promise and incredible possibility, so I continue to check there despite its hopeless track record.

Most often it is my keys that go on mysterious misadventures. One time my wife found them in the trash. Why she thought to look there I don't know but it's just another reason I am lucky to have married her. I check the fridge. She checks the trash. We all have our own oracle and oasis.

After much deliberation, I have concluded that I prefer the term "fanny" in regards to slang terminology for the female derriere. "Caboose" was a strong runner up, but in the end, "fanny" just seems classier, yet with a subtle hint of mischief and innocent eroticism. Fanny.

I have a love/hate relationship with limited edition foodstuffs. Be it my beloved Boo Berry Cereal, the nectar of the gods that ye mortals call eggnog, the now legendary Big Stuf Oreo, or the recently resurfaced Hostess Pudding Pie, I just never seem to fall in love more with something, than that which I know will not last forever. Probably says a lot about me … perhaps too much. I'm not sure if labeling something Limited Edition triggers me to become obsessed, if it's just a self-fulfilling prophecy, or if it's something deeper and perhaps in direct proportion to my secretive inner nature, but when I know time is running out, I go to great lengths to prolong the experience and to try and defy the inevitable. As Captain James T. Kirk once said, "I don't believe in the no-win scenario."

And though fresh eggnog can still only be purchased around the winter holidays, the Big Stuf Oreo has sadly never returned to my super market shelves, and for the most part, Boo Berry Cereal is only widely available around Halloween despite the year-round appearances of Count Chocula, a point I have yet to accept. I did, I think, have success on one front—the Hostess Pudding Pie. Many childhood memories include me sinking my pre-molars into Hostess Pudding Pies, and then, just like virginity on prom night, they were gone. Oh, how cruel the world can seem once your innocence has faded and your belly is empty.

About a dozen years ago, I took up the torch and led a one-man campaign to bring back the Pudding Pie by e-mailing the company that made them, once a day, every day, for a year. (I actually didn't have anything else to do one night at work, and then it became something I did every night at work. Hell, if nothing else, it beat doing work.) I sat there awash in the soft blue glow of the computer screen like Doogie Howser MD, typing sweet prose to Twinkie the Kid over at Hostess, pleading with him to find it within his cream filled heart to reinstate the Pudding Pie into Hostess' starting line-up. I never did receive any letter, e-mail, or confirmation that Mr. Kid was reading my nightly diatribes, probably because he thought I was crazy, but just a few years ago, they did reappear for sale and I would like to think that in some small way it may have had to do with me.

On a strangely related note, I did receive a letter from the Subway headquarters on an official letterhead apologizing for me feeling slighted by their advertising campaign featuring a fellow named Jared. They even sent me some coupons along with the letter. I didn't think the fact that one guy lost weight by eating only at Subway was anything to celebrate, never mind something to advertise.

Also, there was one time that I received a case of Fruit Stripe Gum from the good people at Wrigley's after writing to them about how much I have enjoyed their products over the years. Anyhow, I thought that was nice, but I see I have once again strayed from topic as neither Subway nor Fruit Stripe Gum are limited edition products.

Oh well. I told you I get easily distracted.

Note to my readers: You now know entirely too much about me. Congratulations. I'm sorry.

Happy Birthday, America!
07.04.09

In a lifetime, there are but few precious moments when it seems that the universe itself is conspiring to help you make all the right moves. The times when you are at the store checkout and reach into your pocket to find you have the exact amount of change. The moment you returned to your car just when the meter maid was going to write you a ticket. Or when you come back from the restaurant bathroom just as your meal arrives all hot and tasty like a prom queen. The stars are in alignment, the seas are tranquil, the moon shines a spotlight on your life and everything is at peace. It is as if you bought the world a Coke and taught everyone to sing in perfect harmony.

Being a big proponent of all things happy and pure, and not so much Coke, unless it's the cherry variety, I truly do appreciate these rare and special moments. I look forward to them arriving in their due time. So much so, in fact, that when I start to get a glimmer of one appearing in my own life, I become quite twitterpated—as in the feeling you get when you first catch the eye of that certain someone as beautifully illustrated in the Disney animated classic *Bambi*. Your heart starts to pound, your eyes grow wide, and you almost lose your head. I also get this feeling of twitterpation when I see those oversized multicolored Christmas lights from the 80's shining bravely into the darkness of a cold winter night. They seem to stir up some sort of sexual excitement as well, though I'm not sure as to why.

On July 4th of 2009, the stage was set for precisely one of these all too fleeting moments of perfection. For you see, I had been in South America for nearly a month and I was finally flying home to my loving family in the United States of America, fittingly enough on Independence Day.

I had visions of soaring high above the fruited plains and the purple mountains majesty of my homeland while stewardesses served hotdogs, James Brown sang "Living In America" and I sat triumphantly blazing into the States, a fiery sparkler in each hand. The entire plane full of passengers would be wearing various shades of red, white, and blue, while the pilot and co-pilot would be dressed as Lady Liberty and Uncle Sam. I imagined that I would deplane to a spontaneous chorus of "U-S-A! U-S-A!" and Bruce Springsteen would howl out the lyrics to "Born in the USA" while I awaited the arrival of my luggage at the baggage carousel. This was surely my special day—you could almost smell the freedom and taste the pie.

However, the plane departed Santiago, Chile, with no pomp or circumstance and sadly I must report they routinely served chicken with veggies and no one played "Living In America" or any other James Brown classic. A shame, really. The pilots were in their usual uniforms and the people on the plane were only decked out in their white cotton surgical masks in a vain attempt to avoid whatever the new virus or plague of the week was. I sat there mask-free, feeling like the last cowboy.

What was happening to my America? Where was the pride of returning to the land of apple pie, baseball, and heavy-hootered American women? Mmm ... pie. Where were my fireworks? Surely a sparkler wouldn't blow a plane clear out of the sky. How about at least letting me light a few of those little black snakes in the exit row? A champagne popper of streamers—something—anything?! "Hooray for the red, white, and blue..." was echoing through my mind.

Alas the heartaches continued, when I landed in Atlanta, Georgia, to make my connection. There was no spontaneous chorus of "U-S-A!" Instead there was a line for immigration that might have well had stretched all the way back to South America itself. Son of a -----!

In a lifetime, there are but few precious moments when it seems that the universe itself is conspiring to help you make all the right moves ... however this was not one of those days. The stars weren't in alignment, no one was singing, and there was no Cherry Coke to be had. Stumped again.

I waited with my fellow Americans to show my passport and answer questions about being on farms and smuggling in meat products. I shuffled a step or two every five minutes over a two-hour period. All the time listening to "Roam" by the B-52's as it played in an endless cycle on the overhead customs procedure informational video. Perhaps the producer of this video opus thought himself clever for using the song and its sickening bubblegum chorus to entertain the captive audience in the maddening serpentine line that grew like a black snake that I wasn't allowed to light on the plane. Perhaps the producer was a sadist and knew the effect it would have upon the people who stand solemn, slowly kicking their heavy packs down the way. Perhaps the producer didn't think at all.

By the time I finally reached the immigration agent, the last thing I ever wanted to do again was roam if I wanted to. Roam around the world....

I was quickly waved through to customs, and then again to security and onto another plane complete with a cockpit of disappointment. The pilot meekly mumbled a, "Thanks for flying with us on this holiday weekend," which is the politically safe vernacular that is used to protect the same prissy bastards whom took the Christ out of Christmas and stifled the Pledge of Allegiance in classrooms across this country.

In this strange new world, we are afraid to even slightly offend anyone and will bend to the point of breaking as to make sure everyone is included. We lead our children to believe that there are no winners and no losers. After the game, everyone gets a trophy. Everyone is a special and unique snowflake, just like everybody else.

I found myself floating in a sea of questions, yet squished between a plastic window in the clouds and what would appear to be a mile-high surgical team prepping for another media lobotomy. When did everyone start playing it safe? When did fear grip us to the point of strangulation? What the hell is going on?

I believe in treating people fairly. I believe in treating people with respect. I believe in making suitable accommodations for those with various disabilities. I also believe that people are being coddled to the point of a sociological developmental hindrance and this nonsense must stop or we will lose everything. In the ocean, a school of fish is only as fast as its slowest member. On land, we have been catering to our slowest members for much too long. We will not evolve; a bigger fish will simply eat us all.

I was near my wits end when I calmly reminded myself that regardless of what is going on in the world, regardless of my interpretation of it, regardless of my dislike of it, my day would still end fantastically as my family would be there to greet me at the airport, even if they were not accompanied by a spontaneous song and dance number about the American way. Maybe I simply set my sights too high. Maybe I should stop wishing my life to be a musical. Maybe the United States I grew up in was simply a fading distant memory. Perhaps surgical masks, hand sanitizers, and politically correct verbiage were the new face of this land I love; a face frozen in fear and sadness like a botched Botox treatment.

Then I looked over at the woman sitting across the aisle from me. She was reading a copy of *USA Today*, and there on the cover was the Statue of Liberty. The article proclaimed that her mighty crown was once again open for the public to climb up into and look out over the sea or back to the harbor of New York for the first time since the cowardly attacks that took place on September 11th.

Majestic Lady Liberty was back and as beautiful as ever. America! Hell yeah!

Note to my readers: Well, here we are. As I write this I must say that the land that I love is still a bit wonky and getting stranger all the time. Sadly, too many look upon our differences rather than our commonalities. And differences are not in themselves a bad thing either. I view differences as God's unique fingerprints upon us all. I view my race as "human". My religion is "kindness and love". These titles are applicable to us all and they allow for a lot of understanding. All good things. All good things.

And I apologize for use of the term "heavy-hootered" in the essay. I'm a sucker for alliteration. As it would turn out, I have matured into more of a fan of a lady's fanny anyhow. Ah, well. We all have our things.

What Is Really Going On?
07.28.09

So here we are, in the midst of an economic depression, recession, or whatever the media is calling it this week. Joblessness is on the rise, the housing market has fallen apart, many people that we know, and maybe even you yourself, are in danger of losing everything they/you have. We are unable to pay bills, unable to make ends meet, and more importantly, unable to see what has caused this disturbing reality.

How did we get to this point? How is it that a year ago almost everyone could afford a home, everyone could pay their bills, and they were still making cars in Detroit? Yet now, everything seems turned upside down. Do you blame the banks? Do you blame the mortgage lenders? Do you blame the government? Surely all parties had a hand in this economic downswing, though everyone will claim innocence. However, what is it that caused these dirty angels to act the way they did?

Greed. The influence of evil forces within our very world brought to us by those who walk amongst us, masquerading as co-workers, friends, and media moguls. If you do not believe there is an unseen or "invisible" war going on between the forces of good and evil, then perhaps you should be looking a bit closer. The lust for money and material possessions in this life has caused plastic people to act in ways that have done seemingly irreparable damage to the way of life as we know it; a dark scar on the face of our times. Yet, how could these seemingly good and decent people, appointed to positions of management and offices of control, suddenly turn so dark, so cold and so careless?

It seems that it wasn't such a sudden change but a mere constant erosion, almost undetectable by even the victims themselves. No one starts out wanting to be the bad guy. It's rather a small, almost miniscule series of steps that eventually leads to a darker being. You start by taking just a little extra for yourself, surely no one else will miss it, and after all, it's not like you are really hurting anyone. Surely there are people much more sinister than you committing much more heinous acts. That's what the evil forces want you to think of. They want you to compare your misdeeds with the larger wrong doings of others. Erosion starts slowly but gains speed quickly.

Compared to murdering someone, stealing a few things from the office isn't so bad, is it?

The blurring of the line in between right and wrong is an underlying problem within our society. It is imperative that we keep in mind that there is no gray area in God's truth. All too often we are susceptible to this moral decay that is slowly eating away at our very foundation, until it is too late and we are simply swept away in the destructive current of sin and moral ambiguity.

So how do we fight back? How do we do our part in this struggle between the unseen forces of the heavens? We need to be people of discernment. We need to be aware of erosion and the unseen forces that influence our times and ourselves. We need to reject the basic assumptions of civilization, especially the importance of material possessions. All that glitters is not gold, and gold itself is only as valuable as you think it is.

As it is written in Ephesians 4: 22-24, we must lay aside the old self that is corrupted with desire and deceit and lust for material things and clothe ourselves with the new nature, which was created according to God's image in righteousness and true holiness. We need to be God's chosen people who can not only see what is happening in the world around them, but are also able to see why these things are happening, and to raise up against these immoralities. We need to be warriors of light and love and live our lives as thus. Good because we are good, not good because of comparison.

God bless us all. Regardless of which deity you may or may not subscribe to.

Note to my readers: I don't have much to add. This is still very much how I see things. I will say that I also am not perfect by far, so please do not think I am preaching from an ivory tower. I am a damn mess at most times, but I keep going forward and trying to do what is right. I stumble. I fall. I make mistakes. But I keep trying.

Apocalypse How?
January 2012

People ask me all the time if I worry about the 2012 prophecy. Were the Mayans really onto something? Is it the end of times? Do we have any hope? I have researched it, I have looked deeply into its significance and how the date relates to other enigmatic facets of different cultures, rituals, beliefs, sages, madmen, and various doomsday prophets. Is the veil thinning? Is there a rag-tag band of demons just standing in line, listening to their iPods, waiting, as the date grows increasingly closer? Is any of this 2012 stuff a significant thing to be concerned with in the least?

Well, let us take a look and see:

The fact that our good friends at NASA have expressed their own curiosity with the date in regards to the alignment of a black hole with the center of our galaxy, while the Earth is in alignment with the sun, a galactic event that takes place only once every 25,800 years, that raises my eyebrows. They do not know what the result of this may be. It could be a dramatic change in the world and in life as we know it. It could be a subtle, yet catastrophic shifting within the magnetic polarization of the earth that would take years to complete. It could, and most likely will be, nothing at all.

Also, there was a recent study at Princeton that has garnered evidence to suggest the magnetic poles of the Earth may have shifted before. The fact that Albert Einstein proposed a theory like Pole Shift back in 1955 gives me pause, as I do respect anyone with an outlandish hairstyle.

Every generation has its moments when people think, "The end is near!" but could it really be it this time? In the great galactic doomsday lottery, do we hold the ticket with the final numbers on it? I doubt it. I never win the lottery.

In Biblical times, when Jesus died and was resurrected from the dead, there were many people whom believed He would return in their lifetime and that would be the end of days. Yet here we are, so many years later, still waiting.

In 1999, The Artist Formerly Known as Prince, and then known as Prince again, enjoyed a brief resurgence of his earlier hit as many people did indeed party like it was 1999. However, sadly, in cold musty basements and shoddily constructed bomb shelters across the globe, sat those who did not party at all. Instead, they counted down the last moments of humanity surrounded by wooden pallets, stockpiled high with canned vegetables, Spam, Twinkies, and bottled water, waiting for planes to drop out of the sky and for their toaster oven to turn into a rabid killing machine; all because of some silly computer programmers and their binary world literature was coupled with yet another loosely interpreted Nostradamus prediction fueled by such captivating and factual reporting by the staff of the now defunct *Weekly World News*. (Side note: I love the *Weekly World News*. Long live Bat Boy!)

And now, here we are, still standing, and defiantly staring down yet another apocalypse.

So, what do I think about the 2012 prophecy? I find it intriguing. I find it more plausible than the other end game scenarios that have been presented. Yet, I am not terribly concerned with it. Instead, I am more concerned with the blatant disregard mankind is showing for each other in these troubled times.

Earthquake after earthquake, tsunamis and hurricanes, flooding and wild fires; yet, all we are concerned with is ourselves. Sure, we donate some money, on Twitter we retweet the phone number to help the victims. Then we go back to our lives, our Facebook accounts, our iPhones and our distraction. Never looking at the big picture. Never stopping to change the ways in which we live our hurried, egocentric, isolated lives. Never looking up from our text messaging to see the young child crossing the road. Never taking a break from our reality shows to see that in reality our neighbor is in trouble. Never stopping to help the girl in the street as she is brutally beaten by others. Never looking at our own lives and seeing how, even in some small way we can initiate change. Never seeing that we are all in this together; that all are one. That we need each other, that we need hope, that we need faith, that we need miracles, and that a life without these things that I have mentioned means we shall surely perish despite ourselves, in 2012, or at some other time.

For a society living in a time where there are so many ways to communicate, not much that truly matters is being said. We are LOL-ing. We are sexting. We are taking overhead photos of ourselves at arm's length as we stand there in our underwear for the entire world to see our shame. We are friends with so many, yet utterly alone as we care for only ourselves.

In regards to the end of time, there is one report I have read that I have complete faith in. It is full of prophets, full of celestial beings, full of predictions. Even as it pertains to what is going on today, it seems right on target. It's the Bible. And though Jesus never gave us an exact date like our friends the Mayans have, He did say it would happen, and that if we have our spiritual houses in order we have nothing to fear.

So, do I worry about the 2012 prophecy?

Nah … I simply live in faith, not in fear. God bless.

II
INTERNATIONAL TRAVELS UNRAVELED

The Day That Never Was
03.11.08

Traveling to New Zealand from New England is no easy feat. Traveling to England from New Zealand is even worse, but let's not put the rickshaw before the man, so to speak. In order to get to New Zealand from Rhode Island, you first must travel to Logan Airport in Boston and make your way to the plane. This is more difficult than it seems; you would know this if you have ever attempted to get onto an international flight out of Beantown.

Circuitous lines and luggage carousels dart the landscape of what is sure to be a traveler's hell or a mean-spirited purgatory in the very least. Having navigated the check-in line like Columbus searching for a trade route to India, I had finally arrived at the counter and encountered an Indian of my own; think red dot, not feather. The language barrier, despite his heart-felt attempts at English, seemed to hinder our transaction. This surely was daunting foreshadowing for my trip, since I was about to travel internationally for over a month and there I was unable to communicate within my own little territory on this spinning rock of ever evolving madness. He was a very kind gentleman, clean cut and polite, with a thick swatch of dark hair atop his head like a lost patch of nighttime sky. My attempts to explain my path to New Zealand by way of San Francisco and then onward to England seemed to puzzle him, but he assured me not to worry, he would get it all figured out if I would just proceed to gate such and such. I tipped my cap to my new friend and descended deep into the security checkpoint labyrinth.

I was able to elude the first porter, which chastises and questions you about your on-board liquids. I wanted to assure her that the only liquids I was packing were a bladder full of recycled beer and a sac full of freshly produced man seed; but then I knew I was only inviting an unwanted inquiry as to how many ounces of each I had on my person, and the end result would have been a very awkward explanation to my wife about why I was forced to "drop trou" and masturbate at Logan Airport in order to be in compliance with FAA regulations. (Damn terrorists. As if taking off everyone's shoes was not inconvenient enough.)

After taking out my laptop, removing everything from my pockets, and leaving my humility, dignity and pocket change on the X-ray conveyor, I was finally free to board the plane and begin my journey.

Planes are an interesting medium in which to travel. The sheer science of flying is hard enough to understand; but I am more curious as to the mathematical equation the airline uses to determine exactly how many crazy people are allowed on the plane at one time. Aboard every flight that I have been on there has been at least one person who is clearly a few fries short of a Happy Meal. Luckily for me, on this six-and-a-half-hour trip, the crazy person must have been bumped up to business class in some strange marketing strategy by the airline, as I am happy to report my flight was comfortable, quiet and uneventful.

Of course, in the give and take of life, the yin and yang of the cosmos, the ebony and ivory of Paul McCartney's piano, eventually the worm turns and it's time to pay the piper. My piper was a raving madman with large Larry King spectacles and two-row halitosis. I know this because I was seated two rows in front of him and still could not escape his troubled, tic-tac free breath for the full twelve-hour flight. He was quiet during the flight, but takeoff and landing procedures proved to be a great hurdle for this mental athlete.

Per the new FAA regulations, the flight crew will ask you to open your window shades upon takeoff and landing. I am not sure as to why this must be done, as it never was an issue before. I assume it is just so we can all have a clear view of our twisted and fiery deaths should something go horribly wrong. Regardless of the real reason I blindly comply, since, outside of one short flying lesson, I have no formal flight training.

The same could not be said however of my bespectacled traveling companion whom is apparently an ace of the skies in his own storm-clouded mind. He starts jamming the shade up and down violently while loudly questioning the policies, procedures and the integrity of the airline. Now don't get me wrong, I am all for challenging authority when I think there are fights to be fought and battles to be won. When it comes to little things like opening my window shade, I choose to be a good little Christian soldier and play ball.

The stewardess was coming over to settle him down when he randomly shifted gears and started complaining about shutting down the in-flight entertainment while we were still technically "in flight". She tried to explain about the guidance systems and such when he claimed that the business class passengers were still watching the movie and we were being segregated because of our "financial brackets and placement within the plane." The stewardess, realizing this man was flying in his own unfriendly skies, turned and left the man without further answers. I was expecting him to break into the protesting classic, "Hell no, we won't go!" at any moment, when he suddenly opted for a quiet sit-in demonstration instead.

I dozed off for the landing and woke up in Auckland, New Zealand. This was once again not my final destination, as I had to then hop a seemingly short two-hour flight to Dunedin, New Zealand.

Getting your luggage at an airport is always a game of chance, a twist of fate, and a toss of the coin of life. It always starts out the same, full of hope and dreams; like a child before they find out you truly can't be whatever you want to be. We want to think that but there are certain insurmountable limitations. Then there is that moment when you start seeing the same bags repeatedly and yours is not among them. Like a twisted merry-go-round of bad one night stands haunting your memory and there you are, forced to watch and powerless to stop it. Suddenly one bag pops through the luggage chute like a baby from the rubber airport vagina and someone runs up to claim it; a smile upon their face like a child on Christmas morning. Life is good and all is right with the world.

Standing alone at the baggage carousel in Dunedin, I was surrounded with people who were all getting what they wanted for Christmas. Apparently, Santa thought I was a bad boy. I hung my head in utter defeat. After over twenty hours of traveling it became abundantly clear that my bags had not made the same journey I did. It appeared that my Indian friend back in Boston was unable to straighten things out after I proceeded to the gate so many hours ago.

My baggage had become a casualty; hopelessly discarded along the roadside of life like an unwanted Christmas tree on December 26th.

Perhaps my luggage was caught up in some time space continuum rift like in the *Twilight Zone*. After all, we did cross the international date line during our flight, which had left me without the experience of what March 11, 2008, may have held for me. Maybe that was the day I would have won the lottery; I will never know for sure.

The only thing I did know was that I was in New Zealand without any pants and the trip had just begun.

Chocolate Poison with a Touch of Maori Clarity

My first stop was in Dunedin, New Zealand. People seem enamored with the place because *Lord of the Rings* was filmed there. I had never seen the movies nor read the books, so the magic was lost to me.

As I cruised the foreign land, I took in the scenery from the stiff seat of the transport van. There really isn't much else to do and the ride was long, so you might as well have a look around. The landscape itself was pleasing. Just outside of the town there were lots of grassy knolls, lush hillsides, and valleys all dotted with sheep; as if God dropped an entire bag of cotton balls out of his heavenly medicine cabinet upon his green bathroom rug. I would imagine he has the softest of quilted toilet paper. That must be a pleasant experience for one's captain's quarters. I was picturing New Zealand to be more like the landscape I had seen in the *Crocodile Dundee* movies of the 80s. I was expecting rivers and desert flats with, of course, crocodiles and kangaroos. I suppose the Australian outback is a bit different from the college town of Dunedin, New Zealand.

I arrived at a very non-descript hotel and quickly ran inside to take a hot shower and return the bladder gauge to empty. Hot showers are one of the basic necessities that I require in order to feel comfortable after an epic travel event. And this, being my first week of what would prove to be many away from home, I needed as many creature comforts as possible. I was already missing my family and wondering if leaving them to film a reality show was really the best thing to do in my reality. Though I am a devout member of the Catholic tribe, I am also a big believer in fate and destiny. I needed a sign. I needed something from the Big Guy upstairs to tell me that I was doing the right thing.

I soft-shoed it out of the hotel and ankled it around the corner to see what a little lost American could find that might bring him some comfort. That's when, as Ace of Base once sang, "I saw the sign." Located directly around the corner from my hotel was the Cadbury Chocolate factory! It was as if my intergalactic travel agent had booked me a trip to Wonka-Land at last. Screw you Charlie Bucket, D. Pari has a golden ticket of his own, and he will not be stealing Fizzy Lifting Drink, thank you very much.

The Cadbury factory proved to be quite the treat. Floor upon floor of chocolaty goodness all layered up like a giant crème egg and I was at the yolk of it all. Every time we stopped at a new part of the factory they rewarded you with the chocolate bar that is made there.

I had Dairy Milk Bars, Perky Nanas, and even some cocoa beans straight out of the jungle; or at least out of the little bucket under a fern placed there to make it feel jungle-esque. It was all very convincing to my inner-child who was floating very near the surface now. At the end of the tour was a chocolate waterfall, which was more of a huge bucket of chocolate being dumped down the middle of a storage silo. But it was, in essence, the closest thing to a chocolate waterfall I would probably ever see, so I didn't mind suspending disbelief for a moment.

The best part of staying at a hotel close to a chocolate factory is that during the day they open the windows and the enticing aroma of chocolate fills the air and teases the nostrils like the sweet perfume of your seventh grade crush as it escapes the tightly pulled fibers of her plush white sweater.

The worst part of staying at a hotel close to a chocolate factory is that during the day they open the windows and the enticing aroma of chocolate fills the air and teases the nostrils like the sweet perfume of your seventh-grade crush as it escapes the tightly pulled fibers of her plush white sweater.

I became a cocoa bean junkie. Every day I needed more chocolate. I couldn't make it outside of the hotel without stopping to buy a chocolate bar, sometimes three or four. I pictured myself on a *Reality Stars: Where Are They Now* special some twenty years in the future, sitting there with a smudge of chocolate on my chubby face, a shiny wrapper in each dimpled hand as I bellowed from the fathomless depths of my jelly belly, "I had it all until I went to Dunedin." When the week had finally passed, I ate my last Coconut Rough block of chocolate and bid a thankful farewell to Dunedin and a very obese and troubled vision of my future self.

Traveling on to Wellington I was treated to what some say is a rare event in New Zealand. A welcoming ceremony was to be done by the native Maori tribe. I was told that I was to prepare a song to sing as well as a brief story about myself that would denote who I was and what I believe in and stand for. The entire ride to the tribal lands I sat contemplating what to say and what to sing. I am far from shy, so performing would not be a problem; but what song to grace them with was a conundrum.

I have always been partial to The Beatles and weak in the knees for Elvis, but then again, who wasn't? I envisioned singing "What a Wonderful World" by Louis Armstrong as that has always held a special place in my heart, but at the same time, it just didn't seem to say what I was about. I toyed with the idea of singing "Juicy" by Notorious B.I.G., though a white guy saying that this song went out to "all the n****s in the struggle" would never go over well, no matter how much I personally, and whole-heartedly felt the sentiment for all those going through hard times.

Suddenly it hit me. I notice things never tend to sneak up quietly and dawn upon me in a pleasant fashion like waking up to breakfast in bed, which is truly one of life's greatest pleasures and one of the most adoring signs of true love. No, with me it's always suddenly. Fast and furious like a Monday morning sports highlight reel. I wonder if that speaks to my psyche or if it's just that I live in a faster mental state then others. I decided it wasn't really that important, breakfast or sports highlights, the important thing was that I had my story and my song. I would talk about my wife, our daughter, and our family. I would sing a song that I had written for our daughter. It was all coming together now, a moment of clarity after a cocoa binge induced euphoric daze. At last I finally knew what it truly meant to be "Coo-coo for Cocoa Puffs". That poor bird, people had him all wrong. I understand, Sonny! I understand.

The most important thing to me is that I am a family man. A small token to some, but in today's "what happens in Vegas stays in Vegas" mentality, I think an honorable man who prides himself on his faithfulness to his family and his ability as a father is something to be proud of. As John Lennon so wonderfully penned, "A working class hero is something to be."

In my mind's eye, which is thankfully not as near sighted as my other ones, I envisioned the Maori tribe as fierce looking warriors with white paint shining like starlight from their midnight skin. Meanwhile, within the always-animated chamber of my inner most thoughts, I kept replaying those old Bugs Bunny cartoons where he was given a bath in a large black pot with carrots bobbing to the boiling surface. I sir, would be no one's dinner, thanks to years of careful Saturday morning study of said cartoons.

The travel van skidded up the dirt road to the sacred tribal meetinghouse. Feeling confident in my plan of song and story, I strode out upon the loose sand and up the path. Lo and behold, there stood what I can only describe as a mulatto-skinned gentleman in Dockers and a Polo shirt. I rubbed my eyes in confusion. Perhaps I had gotten off at the wrong stop. Where were the warriors, the face paint, and the bath cauldron? It appeared technology and modern ways have caught on even with the Maori people. Stumped again! The whole world has gone commercial just as Charlie Brown had feared it would.

One thing I found unique was the traditional greeting which is also called "the sharing of breath". Instead of shaking hands, you place your foreheads together and squish noses. It was very different from anything I have ever experienced before and I found myself thankful for not having that extra helping of garlic bread at lunch.

After being welcomed into the meetinghouse the stage was set for my introduction. Unfortunately, I had arrived late and the musical portion of my performance had been edited from the program due to time constraints. After sharing my tale, I listened to theirs and was quite intrigued to learn how important the family unit was to the Maori people and how they were adapting to change. It was not lost upon them how the world has evolved/mutated and with it their people. In response, they have embraced an increased focus on the importance of family and working together, relying on each other and looking out for the greater good. One point that I personally feel very strongly about is that we should not be focused upon our own lives in this world, rather we should strive to realize what the effects are upon the world because of our lives.

There comes a time when we need to put down our iPods, stop searching for our fifteen gigabytes of fame on YouTube, and really think about what it is we are doing here and what type of legacy we are leaving behind for our children and for all mankind.

The Maori prepared a fine dinner, offered an overnight stay within the meetinghouse, and in the morning a traditional breakfast; which, luckily for me consisted in part of Rice Krispies. I just can't start my day without the sugar-smothered yelps of Snap, Crackle and Pop. I love you crispy, delicious bastards!

After breakfast, I climbed back into the transport van like a pregnant woman onto a donkey, very carefully and a bit tired of traveling so uncomfortably. Not to mention after several days of ten-hour travel the van started to smell a little like the aforementioned beast of burden.

The odorous van pointed its hood toward Wellington, and the bow of the boat that took me from the South Island to the North Island did the same. On a personal note, I keep my bow pointed towards Jesus as He has never give me any reason to believe that He isn't just as good, if not better, than any Global Positioning System that science has produced. Sure, He may not always point out some of the seedier attractions along my travel route, but He does ensure me that I will someday arrive at my destination in a safe manner. It's a long road to Heaven and it's important to make sure you sign up with a good guide.

As it was so well noted in Tarantino's theatrical masterpiece *Pulp Fiction*, the biggest thing one notices when traveling abroad is the little differences. Specifically, I noticed the changes in strategy by the advertising industry. For example, say you are at a gas station in the United States and you want a sweet, succulent fruit flavored treat. Starburst leaps to mind as the leading candy chew. However, say you experience the same desire while at a gas station in New Zealand, you would find the wrapper proudly proclaims "Starburst Sucks". Hmm … and you would think they would have tested this on focus groups. Obviously, they refer to chewy candies such as these as "sucks"; regardless of your opinion of them. Starburst was just the tip of the iceberg, and speaking of icebergs, let's talk penguins.

Various foodstuffs such as potato chips, cookies, and candy bars feature penguins on their packaging for no apparent reason. It seemed a bit confusing that in a land where the official bird is a Kiwi, and the people refer to themselves as Kiwis, you would think the dapperly attired penguin would be runner-up for loveable animated character; however, this is not the case, and thus the penguin proudly struts his stuff down the aisles of Kwiki-Marts throughout the land.

The penguin does not win my award for zany advertising however. That prestigious achievement is reserved for the good doctor. Dr Pepper, that is. Dr Pepper takes the cake with their care free, catchy slogan of, "Dr Pepper–What's the worst that could happen?" complete with twist-off cap that reads "Open by hand," just in case you thought that your butt cheeks may have been the more appropriate tool with which to access the tantalizing, thirst quenching refreshment. After all, what's the worst that could happen?

I was experiencing some lower end pains of my own and thus was very pleased when the tired old transport van slowed its roll at the hotel in Wellington. I needed more than a hot shower to recuperate from my latest travels and so after belting out a rousing chorus of the *Grease* musical medley under hot droplets of sweet salvation, I kissed my nightstand photo of baby and wife and boarded the first train to Sleepy Town, population me.

Funny thing about being on the road—you sometimes wake up not knowing where you are, what day it is, what time zone you are in, or even what month it is. One thing that you can never ever figure out is what the day will bring next.

I started my day with a long stretch and headed out for a jog. I find jogging in new places a bit of an adventure. Some adventures end before they begin and thus was the case with this one.

Downstairs in the lobby I came upon one of my compatriots who excitedly introduced me to Big John from the popular reality television series *Rock of Love* featuring Bret Michaels from Poison, who, in my opinion, was the hardest rocking band of the 80s and is still one of my favorites to this day. As it turns out we watch each other's shows and were equally excited to meet one another. Introductions were made throughout the groups and we were treated to a concert later that week.

I could not have been more pleased with the way things were turning out. It appeared that every time I became a bit down and questioned my methods of providing for my family, I was once again given a sign that I was on the right track. Meeting the band was great, the guys were all cool and we spent a bit of time over the next few nights buying each other drinks and talking. It was as if I were a teenager again. I could almost feel my jean jacket upon my shoulders with the huge Poison logo emblazoned on the back and various band pins on the front. Oh 1980s! Why did it all have to end so soon?

Our tickets for the concert were top notch. We were right down in front where you can almost hear the pluck of the strings just before they squeal through the amplifiers and pierce your ears as you stand there swaying, hypnotized underneath hot neon stage lights glowing with the ferocity of passion that only hair bands could bring. Truly this was a night to be remembered. A night where my inner child was allowed to stay up well past his bedtime, and in doing so rocked his friggin' socks off.

In-Flight Pajamas and Not So Southern Fried Chicken

It was time to fly to jolly ol' England, the land of my ancestors and those of so many others. From New Zealand to England, via California, is over a whole day of flying, so I feel that it is beyond very important that one remain comfortable for such a flight.

For me that means flying while comfortably suited in my in-flight pajamas. This time I sported my festive snowman pajama pants along with coordinating soft cotton, blue snowflake top. I don't care what the fashion police may say, when you are in the air for over 24 hours, you can bet your sweet behind that D. Pari is flying in his jammies.

I have been to England many times before, and I hate to say it, but outside of the beautiful countryside, London nightlife, and the various tourist traps, I find it very tough to get along. My troubles mostly are due to my tongue. I am not referring to its rather short stature or its inability to roll and such, rather I am referring to its unfortunate ability to find any food in England tasty. It appears to me that anything I eat in England, be it a fancy restaurant or chain food, it all has that new car scent taste; rubbery and plastic-like. I'm sure religious freedom and taxation were good reasons to leave the motherland and get over to the States, but I like to think my personal ancestors left mainly for the food.

What I found quite interesting upon this trip to England was my time spent in Wales. I traveled through there on my way to the ferry that would safely shepherd me to the green, green fields of Ireland. I can only describe the landscape of Wales as that of my fairytale dreams. There were rolling hillsides, winding rivers and crooked, dried up trees that stood defiantly like the twisted spine of an old man. I had a few hours to kill before boarding the ferry to Ireland and so I set out in search of something to put in my empty belly. Funny thing about the port town of Wales on a Friday afternoon; there are several open barbershops, but only two open restaurants.

The one I chose advertised "Southern Fried Chicken", which to me was an oasis within a veritable wasteland of unpalatable foodstuffs. And of course, as with any other oasis, be they in my animated world or in the real one, it was too good to be true. My "Southern Fried Chicken" dish with side salad was much less than what was to be desired. Swing and a miss! This was clearly not fried chicken in any hemisphere, be it Southern or Northern. It was more of an oven baked chicken dish, which to its own merit, was quite tasty, even if it was not as advertised.

I had asked the waitress for my accompanying side salad to which she asked if I wanted another. Apparently the one piece of Romaine lettuce with tomato wedge and cucumber slice that I mistook for garnish was the actual salad. Stumped again.

I know it seems like a minor thing, but after five weeks on the road, the idea of a big salad and southern fried chicken become your saving grace. By this point the hotel room has become a prison and any comforts are welcome ones. And when those things that you look to as a life raft reveal themselves to be a Trojan horse, let's just say you get pushed a little bit over the edge.

Thankfully Ireland was on the horizon and though I have no "In-Cruise" pajamas for the ferry ride, I was sure there was a pot o' gold at the end of my rainbow, or at least a bucket of Kentucky Fried Chicken.

Dough and Breadsticks: Two Things I Was Denied in England

"Back in the U.K.-U.K." was not a song the Beatles ever bothered to write, and I am starting to see why.

I had been back in England for two whole days, and due to hotel logistics and time constraints, I was yet unable to change my American currency into Pounds. Without money or sustenance I was starting to shed a few pounds of my own. Neither of which was making me a happy boy with a song in my heart and sunshine in my eyes. Learning from Napoleon's failed attempt at fighting a two-pronged war, I decided to prioritize my problems; first I would go to the bank and then I would find something suitable to eat. If nothing else, having money in my pocket would allow me to buy food, which is probably easier than risking a "dine and dash" in a foreign country and angering the Queen.

After a brisk walk under a grey sky that reminded me of the late Jerry Garcia, I made my way to what Mr. Scrooge and Mr. Marley might lovingly refer to as a "money changing hole". The rest of us not living in a Charles Dickens novel would call it a bank. I approached the teller unaware of with whom I had the pleasure of addressing, Mr. Scrooge or Mr. Marley.

I pleaded my case and put four hundred U.S. notes on the counter between us. The man pushed the money back towards me and said that they only change currency on Mondays. I recalled the late great Mama Cass bellowing, "Monday, Monday, can't trust that day," but at least she was well fed; me, I would kill for a ham sandwich right now.

Finding this preposterous I inquired as to why they wouldn't change it for me today. I reviewed for him the situation as I saw it: we were in a bank, they clearly had money there, he and I were both standing on the appropriate sides of the counter, and so it seemed as logical a time as any for this transaction to take place within the cosmos. He simply replied that they change money on Mondays and today was not Monday.

As it turned out, I had the pleasure of addressing Mr. Scrooge who had not yet had his Yuletide visits, nor had he purchased anyone a Christmas Goose. There would be a tiny crutch propped up against a well-tended to gravestone, and if I didn't get money to buy food soon, the name upon it would read "D. Pari." I could see the inscription: "Here Lies a Man for Whom Monday Never Came,

Despite His Pleading and Logic, He Died Just the Same".

To thwart this macabre vision brought to me by the Ghost of Christmas Future and by viewers like you, I took a moment to recall a similar happening from my life just weeks before. There clearly would be no changing of money here until Monday, so I thought it best to distract myself.

Two Weeks Earlier

When we last left our hero, he had found himself with an empty belly and matching pockets in a town just north of his current location (strange how history repeats itself even when it's just a few weeks old). I had found a bank and was told that they did not change money at all and that I would have to find a Post Office.

Ah yes, the Post Office! Of course! The natural choice when it comes to all things financial. I can only imagine where you have to go to mail letters in this town. Here's a hint: the guy there probably asks you to bend over as he slowly slips a cold rubber glove upon his hand. Mailing letters is a real pain in the ass.

I once heard a joke about Post Offices. They were the only place where they hang up pictures of criminals so you can apparently write letters to them if you so desire. Let's face it, if they were really trying to capture them they would put their pictures on the stamps so that postmen and women alike could look for them while they delivered the mail each day.

Back to jolly ol' England and my present situation, I realized that maybe here too, I could change money at the Post Office. It was my only hope. I checked my internal compass and made a beeline, which really doesn't make sense if you have ever taken the time on a sunny afternoon to peer over the straw in your wine cooler and watch the circuitous flight pattern of the striped sting-fellow, you would have noticed that a "bee-line" is anything but the shortest possible route. Their own GPS system must constantly be recalculating.

Standing in line, I become nervous as to whether they too subscribed to the "Monday only" mentality of the bank across the way. Most the people in front of me were just buying stamps, though I distinctly heard a gentleman in front of me ask something about a plasma television. After that, I tuned out. Finally, I stood at the front of the line with my head held high and feeling very important. I always feel that making it through the line and achieving the inevitable status of "next" is something to be proud of and admired.

Once at the top of the line I sometimes let people behind me go ahead, just so I can maintain my status, plus I get to make someone else's day just that much better. I don't know why. Perhaps somewhere within the wiring of my deepest and most complex inner workings I like the anticipation of things. Perhaps I like the sense of accomplishment that results in being patient. Perhaps I like to look back at all those behind me and see the disgruntled shadow of the man I once was. Or maybe I am just wired a bit wrong and I find joy in some of the silliest things life has to offer.

I gingerly approached the window and slowly placed my money on the counter as if the police had just told me to put the gun on the ground, while in my mind I was expecting a bullet with "Monday only" written on it to pierce not just the fiber of my jacket but that of my very being as well.

The man behind the window did not flinch and the transaction began. He asked if 180 Pounds was okay. There was a brief shining moment where I thought I had a choice, but before I could mount a response he had taken my 400 dollars. Apparently, we were not going to negotiate. 180 Pounds it was.

In possession of a half empty wallet and a completely empty belly I made my way to a Pizza Hut that I had seen in my travels. Personally, I thought my travels were way more adventurous and entertaining than those of Gulliver despite his notoriety. Perhaps someday school children would be forced to sit in their bedrooms reading the tales of my adventures, whilst their friends call to them from outside as they play beneath a smiling summer sun and animated birds that dance and sing against the background music of the ice cream man's portable dairy orgy of pure joy. That would be my legacy. D. Pari: executioner of summer fun for children. A bunch of sour-faced children missing out on what would in retrospect prove to have been some the most fleeting and joyful days of their lives; as the Earth continues to spin and the calendar continues to countdown to their very extinction. Ah well, I'm sure there would be a Cliff Notes version or some Internet review that they could plagiarize. With every new technology comes a new shortcut and even lazier people. Huzzah! Progress!

Meanwhile, inside the hut of pizza, there stood a sign that said "Please Wait for Service" and who was I to argue with such a polite sign for it did say please after all.

Several minutes later a raven-haired waitress in a flour-smattered uniform made her way over to me. Her smile must have been busy with some other patrons as she stood there before me without it.

I asked for an order of breadsticks for takeout. She replied, "No," and went off to find her smile. We all go off to find something, I thought quietly to myself over the contrasting rumble of my belly.

The sign still said "Please Wait for Service" and since I had not yet received any, and the sign was keeping up its good manners and spirits, I would stick it out and abide by its wishes.

Soon after, a wide smiling, shorthaired gentleman whom looked like every sidekick in every buddy-comedy film you have ever seen approached me. I thought he had enough smile for two people and perhaps he had stolen that of the raven-haired girl. A pity really as she could have desperately used it. I explained to him my desire for seasoned dough cut into rectangular geometrical shapes, or as we call them in America, breadsticks.

He also replied, "No," but instead of turning on his heels and walking into the sunset of the pizza oven, he offered me a large baguette with garlic.

Perhaps it was not what I desired, but sidekick boy was giving me options. I could work with that. I declined the garlic walking stick and further inquired as to my ability, or lack thereof, to purchase breadsticks. He told me that they do not sell them. I stood there perplexed, not due to his reply being incomprehensible, but because I could clearly see them on the buffet table next to the pizzas.

I motioned to the breadsticks thinking that maybe they have a different name for them here in England. He assured me that they were in fact "breadsticks" but that he could not sell me any.

I quickly made an itemized Post-It Note in my head.

The note read as follows:

-Pizza Hut has the necessary ingredients to make breadsticks.

-Pizza Hut prepares breadsticks.

-Pizza Hut serves breadsticks to patrons.

-Pizza Hut will not sell me breadsticks.

-I should further examine my reliance on food products for comfort and joy later.

I discussed my mental Post-It note list with Smiley the sidekick boy and he assured me all items were correct. (Except for that last one, which I felt was rather personal and I did not want to bring him into it. Lord knows there are enough people in my head already.)

Like a good little investigator, I deduced that breadsticks were a "buffet only" item, much like you can only change money at the bank on Mondays, and in some towns, money is like your bitter childhood memory of summer reading, you can't change it at all.

Feeling like a high school teenager who practiced his prom proposal into the wee hours of the night, only to be shot down half way through his awkward, sweaty-palmed presentation to his dream girl, I hung my head and slumped my shoulders and made my way back to the safety of the hotel like a baby, crawling slowly and teary eyed to its mother's sweet, sweet embrace and supple bosom.

Will someone please rock me until I fall asleep, or at least give me a bottle? Rum, not milk. Thank you.

The Lost Liverpool Session Backstory

Sometimes in life, things happen over which you have no control. Most times in life this is how things happen, whether you are aware of it or not, whether you like it or not. Sometimes the story behind the story is an interesting tale in itself.

The date was May 3rd, 2008. I know this because it is imprinted upon the train ticket that is with me at the moment of this writing. The place was Warrington, England. I was there for a spell and decided to take a trip over to Liverpool for the day. On my return trip to Warrington I jotted down notes on the back of the train ticket. These notes were to become a travel log called "The Liverpool Session" and would tell of my time as a day-tripper to the home of The Beatles. However, on my flight home to the States, my luggage was lost and its contents compromised. Not only did I lose many of my personal effects and souvenirs, but I also lost the little ticket stub and thus the material for "The Liverpool Session."

As it were to happen, seven months later, upon my doorstep arrives the lost luggage from its mysterious trip abroad for more than half a year. Upon opening the luggage, I found that not only did my bag go missing but also it had appeared to have an adventure of its very own.

The contents of the once wayward bag were as follows:

One Green Hiking Boot

Ladies' lingerie

Earrings

Jeans

Women's t-shirts

Bed Linens

Notes and memorandums for an office meeting in regards to electronics

Condoms (Not used. Thankfully.)

Condom Wrappers

Obviously, none of the items listed above were mine, but the following items were:

My spare contact lenses

A pair of sunglasses

A guitar pick from The Beatles Museum

A magnet of The Cavern Club–also from The Beatles Museum

And, the lonely train ticket with my writing points

So, after a quick, yet much needed, explanation to my wife and a very thorough washing of my hands, it is now my distinct pleasure to present what is now being called:

The Lost Liverpool Session

"I am he as you are he as you are me and we are all together," are the opening lyrics to "I Am the Walrus", as written by those musical mop-haired giants, The Beatles. The song goes on to say, "sitting on a cornflake, waiting for the van to come," which was running through my mind as I was standing on the platform waiting for the train to come.

The place was Warrington Station and my destination was Liverpool. I was heading to the childhood home of my guitar-slinging heroes. The Beatles have been my favorite musical group since I was in the seventh grade. Something happened that particular year, though I cannot completely put my finger upon it, but somewhere lost in that pubescent haze, I somehow changed and started taking a serious interest in music, and specifically in lyrics.

As a growing boy, who was at the time terribly shy, I was inclined to sing along to their easily understood desires of "I Want to Hold Your Hand". As a thoughtful old soul taking up residence in a young body, I pondered greatly the melancholy "Fool on the Hill". And as an innocent child not yet knowing all the ways of the world, or LSD, I was entranced by the mixture of mysterious lyrics and simple harmonies that were presented by Sgt. Pepper.

The train pulled up to the station and my heart was in my throat. I hadn't been this excited since the first time I laid eyes on my wife, when I saw her standing there; except she was seated at the time. I quickly boarded the train, my own yellow submarine, which would take me to Liverpool. Like Graceland is to Elvis fans, so is Liverpool to Beatles fans. (I am also an Elvis fan, but at the time Graceland is very far away.)

Amazingly, the train was completely empty. I shuffled from one car to the next, thinking there must be a spot where other excited fans were having a small party of sorts, but alas, there was no one. So, I took a seat in the sunshine as scenic English gardens and my own memories rushed by the window of my mind.

My face pressed against the glass like a child in a toy window, the scenery began to blur and I was recalling the time my parents were called in by my teachers for a conference because I would sit in the rear of the classroom and sing while the other students were trying to learn. I always did well in school and found the mundane pace rather boring, and so I would entertain myself. They are the egg men, I am the Walrus- goo goo g'joob.

Feeling a little disheartened in the lonely passenger car, I decided to sing myself a song to lift my spirits and lighten my mood. After all, I have been known to tear up a karaoke bar on occasion. In specific, there once was a Chinese restaurant back home that advertised not only karaoke on Wednesday nights, but also boasted having the "2nd Best Chinese Food." I appreciate that type of honesty, and thus they received my business and displays of vocal "excellence."

So, whilst sitting in the cool air of the morning I dove into my mental song book of favorite tunes and, not being one to waste the God given opportunity of an empty train, I also decided I would record the event for posterity, and thus a little music video of yours truly was filmed singing "Twist and Shout" whilst in transit to Liverpool.

Several stops and strained vocal chords later, more passengers boarded the train and thus derailed my one-man karaoke show. I really wished they hadn't. Not just because of the enjoyment I was having without them there, but also due to the negative energy these people carried with them. These were not Beatles fans going to Liverpool. No, these were worker bees, off to slave for her Majesty. Their emotional baggage was overwhelming; suddenly I felt as if I was on board the bus to fat camp, and the last Snickers bar was melting in the strained pocket of a pair of husky sized jeans.

I decided to stare absently out the window and focus upon my destination. I would not let anything ruin my soon to be treasured memory. To think I would be walking down the same streets that were once crushed under the boot of John Lennon himself. John has always been my favorite Beatle. I liked his outspokenness, his raw charisma, and his cocky attitude. After all, there is nothing wrong with being confident in one's own abilities. However still there are those who are quick to trounce his good name and label him egotistical. Even Bambi had enemies.

When the train finally arrived at Liverpool I found myself awash in a sea of English culture that I have never witnessed in any of my previous trips to the land of the Queen.

I gazed at towering churches with peaks that pierced the clouds. I walked through a bustling shopping district complete with tiny music stores that featured local artists and the like. Liverpool projected a distinct culture that blended a bit of New York City with that of a sleepy seaport town reminiscent of Salem, Massachusetts. You could tell by watching the teenagers move about the streets, that much of what made The Beatles who they were, remain here still today. Flamboyant hairstyles, thrift store clothes, and rebellious attitudes are so numerous that they are the norm despite themselves. Crushing their own individuality and their own revolution. Everyone is different, just like everybody else. Melting snowflakes as far as the eye can see. Many shops and stores had taken to adorning a clever moniker to more closely identify themselves with the sounds of yesteryear and their local heroes. One that I recall was a 99-cent store called "Penny Lane". Well played.

I went to The Beatles Museum and stood in line with the rest of my musical brethren while John Lennon look-alikes worked the crowd to hustle a Pound and appease the masses waiting in the hot sun. Once inside I strolled through the exhibition halls, my eyes like two little near sighted sponges absorbed countless images of the Fab Four at different points in their career. Ticket stubs from early concerts, first pressings of records, letters written in their own hands- and it was all there for me to see. I didn't know it was possible to be nostalgic for a time in which one was never in existence, but how else could I possibly explain it.

At the end of the tour was a solid white piano on a stage by itself. Imagine playing softly in the background on a whimsical loop. Nothing more needed to be written or said.

I headed out through the gift shop and bought my necessary items for friends and family back home. I then asked the cashier for directions to the infamous Cavern Club where the Beatles first played to groups of swooning teenage girls. He reminded me that it was demolished years earlier, which I sadly remembered seeing on the news a long time ago. I recalled that at one time they were selling the very bricks that made up the place to fans around the globe for astronomical prices. Nothing lasts forever, and to quote Chuck Palahniuk, "even the Mona Lisa is falling apart."

As the Sun King was about to settle deep into the cushions of his throne for some golden slumbers, I slowly made my way back towards the train station. My mind was still racing with all that I had seen that day, while my soul was struggling for an inner sense of peace so that I might take a piece of Liverpool with me. Searching betwixt the sloped rooftops and cobblestone streets for my own little slice of Beatlemania that no one else could have, which could never be destroyed.

I thought of John, Paul, George, and Ringo. I thought of my mother who introduced me to their music. I thought of my Uncle who explained what Sgt. Pepper was all about. I thought about my dad who is an Elvis man and how I have also visited Graceland many moons ago. Then I thought about Yukon Cornelius and Hermey the Elf from the old *Rudolph The Red-Nosed Reindeer* Christmas special. Much like The Beatles, Mr. Cornelius and Mr. um …. Elf, headed out on their own course, in search of their own dreams and destinies. Tired of a world where no one ever really gets to be what he or she wanted to be.

The Beatles became more than rock stars, they became more than legends, they became inspirations to millions worldwide. They were a symbol of freedom and independent thought in a time where having a different haircut made you an outcast, never mind having different political views or anything else that may have been of actual importance.

Now, walking the streets of Liverpool are many branches and offshoots of that exact movement. The shabbily clothed and multi-pierced teenagers stomping up and down the sidewalks. That's part of The Beatles legacy.

My inner seventh grader who was entranced by a musical movement that somehow seemed relevant to his own pubescent inner workings. I am part of The Beatles legacy. Hermey the Elf turned Hermey the Dentist. Santa be damned. He's part of that culture too. We all set out to find our own fame and fortune. Fighting against the mold that was set out before us. Each one carving our own distinct and unique path; a small trickle of hope that will evolve into a stream, branching out into the lives of others many years from now, with world changing consequences we will never know. Life flowing within you and without you.

Naming the Store

The sun is setting as I am walking up the back stairs to my house. I can see inside the doorway. My wife is making dinner under the soft glow of the kitchen light. Our daughter is busy throwing all her toys on the kitchen floor and laughing uncontrollably. I stop to look in briefly on my life in third person narrative. It appears he finally has everything that he has ever wanted. With a smile, he rests a hand on the doorknob.

There is suddenly a knock on the door and I bolt upright.

"Housekeeping!" says the foreign maid just outside my door.

I don't care where you travel, the maids are always foreign to that region. It must be a union thing.

"Why did you wake me? I was almost home," is what my soul is screaming, but my throat is dry and the most I can muster is a barely intelligible, "Not now," like a kid starving off his mother's pleas to get out of bed and ready for school.

I too must face the inevitable. I am not even remotely close to home despite the farsightedness of my mind's eye. In reality, I'm in KwaZulu-Natal, South Africa. A dusty old town located just outside the city of Durban. The dirt roads stretch throughout a very little planned town like a clogged artery in the heart of the Dark Continent. The town itself consists of a pharmacy, a small café, an outdoor goods store, a beauty salon and a convenience store so non-descript that no one had even bothered to name it.

And of course, there was the bed and breakfast on Nottingham Road, in which I was staying. Outside of offering the two things in its title, the bed and breakfast offered little more.

So, what do you do when you have a week to spend in the middle of nowhere? I quickly jotted my options upon a yellow mental sticky note.

The note read as follows in my mind:

-Drink myself silly

-Take nasal decongestants and cough medicine until I pass out

-Watch TV—four channels of soccer and one channel of cricket

-Remember the plots to as many episodes of He-Man as possible

-Name the convenience store

My options were limited but I made the executive decision, which technically I was not qualified for, to name the convenience store.

Just for my own benefit of course, as I would not want to disrupt the locals' way of life, nor impose my name upon them.

My first instinct was to give it an ironic moniker such as "The Inconvenience Store" as you would really have to go out of your way to find it in the first place. But then I realized if I named it that quickly it would leave me with still 6 days, 23 hours and 21 minutes to kill. I would have to press on and search for the perfect name, if for nothing else, to numb my mind until I was on a plane headed for home. A little cerebral anesthesia is just what the doctor ordered. Not too much, just enough to dull the pain of missing my family.

Not too long ago I would have simply found comfort with the good Captain Morgan. He and I have sailed the sweet, caramel colored seas of loneliness, boredom, and alcohol experimentation many times before. Most of our adventures were smooth sailing; but a weeklong excursion would surely have ended up on the rocks or at least with me hanging over the side recycling the contents of my stomach.

Plus, since becoming a husband and a father, I have retired my First Mate duties to the Captain and now only go out on short fishing excursions with him once in a while. We were both getting older anyway and we liked to fish.

So, without liquid muse I set out to do some reconnaissance work on the store. I sat myself down in the sun to absorb some rays as well as the feel of the area. Sitting on the clay colored road I observed the store looming like an odd giant against the barren landscape. Like the first kid in class to reach puberty, it clearly did not fit in. To its left was a series of small tin shack homes. The matriarchs of the local families were outside hanging wet clothes in the hot midday sun while fighting with the occasional dust cloud blowing through the area. To the right of the shadowy monstrosity was nothing but another dirty road heading out of town. I started to feel a little sad for the old decaying store. It seemed so lonely.

After what seemed like hours but what was about twenty minutes, I decided to take a walk inside the belly of the beast, peruse the aisles and get a feel for the place. The store was poorly organized, definitely lacking in the decorating art of Feng Shui. Broken down bicycle parts were piled up in a corner. There were some dusty cans of baby formula stacked up next to rusty machetes. Aging cans of soda sat nestled with dented cans of rodent poison. Half opened bags of cereal and dog food intermingled across the floor.

The aging gentleman behind the antiquated cash register was wrinkled and surly as he sat gazing into a static ridden black and white television set; you could hear his bones creak. A small oscillating fan that no longer oscillated rattled and hummed while pushing hot air by his fatigued brow.

I purchased some gum, (it turned out to be stale—surprise, surprise) and then quietly left. I don't even chew gum as a habit, but I felt the need to purchase something to be polite and the gum was the only thing not sitting next to something that could be harmful if ingested.

On my way, out I took note of the other patrons. All of them seemed more than satisfied with the goods the store had to offer. Everyone seemed to get what he or she needed.

I took a seat back on the roadside across the way and watched the stream of customers come and go. As the minutes slowly trickled by, I realized that the store, despite its shortcomings in my American eyes, was pretty much everything that the people here needed it to be. Perhaps I was too tough on the gentle giant. Sure, it wasn't what I was accustomed to, but for the people of Nottingham Road, it was enough. I suppose it didn't need to have a name after all.

I walked back to the hotel, up the squeaky little stairs to my room and lay in bed, the stale pack of gum still in my hand. I thought about being back home. I thought about my daughter. I thought about what I really needed to get by in this life. It may not be much by others standards, but it's more than enough for me, and that's all that any of us can really ask for. Not to be judged by others standards, but to live according to our own. No matter how messy our own aisles may be.

The Mountain and the Rubble

I have never imagined myself traveling to South Africa before. Not that I was avoiding it for any specific reason, but it just never occurred to me that I should be there. So, without any forethought or precise knowledge of the surrounding area I disembarked the plane in Cape Town and set out for adventure.

I was excited to find out that my hotel was not far from the waterfront point where the Indian and Atlantic Oceans meet. This was a huge attraction for me as these rough seas were steeped in pirate legend and history. Many dastardly men were tossed to Davey Jones' locker when the hulls of their ships cracked upon these very waves that now make for a great picture on my digital camera.

Piracy, as fate would have it, was still very popular within the streets of Cape Town. And thus, the surrounding buildings wore a face paint of pointed fencing and razor wire. Even the preschools and kindergartens have their playgrounds blanketed in the stuff. Flesh piercing metal wrapped around the innocence of childhood, trying to protect the young dreamers of this world from its harsh realities for just a little bit longer, like a mother trying her best to keep them small forever by locking them within the warmth and safety of her all too tight embrace.

Modern pirates now strolled the streets in search of their treasures, which, from what I saw, were now buried within the cars of locals and the pocketbooks of unsuspecting tourists.

There was a growing profession here that I hoped word of would never spread to the local hoods back home. It appears that car theft is such a problem that some people make a living watching your car for you while you go and do your shopping, or take pictures of the waves like surely only a goofy tourist would do.

They simply stand on the street and when you park within their view they make their way over and let you know that they are watching your car for you; it's then understood that when you return, should no harm befall your vehicle, you are to pay them.

I did notice several of the guardian fallen angels looking into and through some of the vehicles after the owner was out of sight. I quickly theorized that should they find something more valuable than what they would be tipped, all bets were off.

It reeked of the "protection" racket that many of my distant

Italian relatives had built an empire upon so many years ago, back in the States. The mere thought of which made my stomach rumble for some good Italian fare the likes of which I could only get back in Rhode Island in one of the best, safest neighborhoods in the world, Federal Hill. (Not really. I mean, the food is stellar, but it's not too safe a place.)

Alas I was a long way from my hometown in the Ocean State, but with the growing growl in my tummy competing with the mighty roar of the ocean, I would have to check my charts and maps and set sail for some local vittles as soon as the tides allowed.

I found a place called "Naked," which of course grabbed my attention, as it was no doubt intended to do. They specialized in shakes, smoothies, and wraps; so obviously, I ordered something else. A menu item that intrigued me consisted of fried bananas, crispy bacon, and chili, served up on a bagel. I have never been a chili guy, so I asked for it without the spicy ingredient and awaited my first taste of South African cuisine.

The sheer look of it conjured up images of tastefulness. A toasty brown bagel comforting the soft tan and yellow gel of the fried banana contrasted against the deep red and crimson coloring of the pig meat; this surely was a feast for the eyes. As it would turn out the "Sweet and Spicy" as they called it, tasted even better than it looked. After just one bite I knew that there was no sense in looking further for my favorite place to eat on the southernmost tip of the African continent. Just like the Beatles' album, I too would just "Let It Be—Naked".

Like many major cities across the globe, the beauty of the sprawling metropolis always does its best to hide the imperfections that dwell within the cracks and alleyways of its sprawling masterpiece. I'm sure that if you stood nose to nose with the Mona Lisa she wouldn't look nearly as breathtaking as she does from across the gallery. In many aspects of life, I find it best to enjoy what there is to be enjoyed, and not peek behind the curtain lest you shall find yourself sadly disappointed.

From across the gallery South Africa boasts a mountain that dominates its skyline. They call it "Table Mountain" and it is quite a magnificent site to behold. As you stand at its base, peering up to where it pierces the clouds like a virgin on her wedding night, you can't help but feel like a three-year-old standing at your Daddy's feet, staring up past a large metal belt buckle and feeling terribly small and insignificant.

This was a breathtaking site, truly a great work of whatever god or scientific theory you have subscribed to. But just like dating the hottest girl in school, after you have experienced her sweater encased mountains a dozen times, they lose their luster and magnificent wonder and only then do you realize that beneath those mountains lies an empty and lonely girl full of perversion, a product of a troubled childhood.

Beneath Table Mountain you can see a street littered with discarded stolen purses and dealers of miscellaneous goods. On certain blocks, you will be offered marijuana. In other parts of town people try and sell you "high quality" socks. In one particularly hard to find area was a very time withered man who was selling little tubes of super glue out of the palm of his hand.

You can see stores selling pornography, alcohol, smoking pipes, and even one merchant that was promoting a rubber duck complete with its own rubber manhood. It was surely the ultimate bath toy for the sexually adventurous, fowl aficionado. However, you can find these things in almost any large city, with maybe the exception of the penile enhanced duck, if you bother to look. Most of us decide it is best to just stare up at the mountain. The fantasy of life is often much more enjoyable than the reality that sneaks around beneath it.

I am a bit of an enigma. I am a dreamer. I am a believer. I am a good little Christian soldier though terribly flawed. I am a thankful husband and a grateful father. I am the eternal optimist, yet there is no optimism. I know the true answer to the glass being half full or half empty.

It is merely your own perception that puts you on one side or the other of this age-old question. The truth of the matter is that there exists the perfect amount of liquid, for most of us our expectations and demands upon this life are just too great, and thus, the glass is just too damn big, leaving us wanting more. In life, we have all been supplied with the exact amount of liquid needed to sustain ourselves.

However, it is my firm belief, as well coined in the Tom Cruise movie *Vanilla Sky*, that one cannot truly enjoy the sweetness of this life without experiencing the sour. It is in the spirit of this belief that whilst here in Africa, and in all places I may be in life, I choose to look at both the rocky mountainside and the rubble that stands below it. After all, we all have to be built upon something.

A lot of Cape Town has its heritage steeped in the oceanic trading and voyages of explorers. Cape Town Castle itself was used as a supply destination for many. And just as the pirates and traders who patrolled the waters of the ancient world relied upon explorers for their survival, today, many modern-day robbers, thieves and peddlers rely upon explorers and travelers for the same. Some of them selling weed. Others selling high quality socks. And then there is one man selling super glue, perhaps in the effort to unite the mountain with the rubble.

My Convoluted Slovakian Memories

Since I was going to Slovakia for the first time, I quickly breezed through my internal card catalog to see what knowledge I had of the land. Three things leapt to my mind like the opening scene in *Bambi* when all the animals are scurrying and scampering about, right before Bambi's mother and my childhood innocence were shot dead right there on the big screen; popcorn falling about the floor of the theater and my mind, soaked in blood and butter.

First on the list of Slovakian reference materials was that I could briefly recall doing a Social Studies report on Czechoslovakia for my fifth grade history teacher, Mrs. Rowley. I remember her being a short woman with glasses and a strict teaching style. The other kids may have resented her for it but I admired it. Moreover, I respected the significant change from the constant coddling of the lower grades I had traversed before. I hated only being as fast as our slowest fish when I was in a classroom with several one-finned wonders. Finally, we were being treated as unique individuals with different learning abilities and disabilities. Being in fifth grade was serious business.

In my school (lovingly nicknamed "Our Lady of the Dollar Sign" by my best friend and lifelong co-conspirator, Darren Valedofsky), being in the fifth grade meant you were on the second floor of the building, you had to change classrooms throughout the day, you ate lunch with the big kids, and occasionally, the principal would call upon you when folding chairs needed to be carried and set up in the auditorium. Grunt work child labor at its finest, my first taste of the real world.

Fifth grade was specifically significant for me as it was the year I ditched the bowl haircut and never looked back. I was done being Moe of Three Stooges; which was fine with me as I was always a Curly man anyway.

Out of all things I remembered about being in fifth grade, apparently the report on Czechoslovakia was not the most important. Outside of the crudely drawn outline of the country that I had sketched on gray construction paper, I could recall nothing else. The drawing did not even come complete with neighboring countries. It was just a gray country floating in a gray sea of nothingness, a dark abyss where not even hope or tweeting cartoon birds could escape.

Strike one.

Second on the list of Czechoslovakia related information that had been filed upon the dusty shelves of my mind's library, was that when I used to play my ice hockey video game on the ol' Nintendo, I would always use the Czechoslovakian team for my own. Once again, they were portrayed in the color gray and were crudely drawn, but it was the time of 8-bit graphic cards and I am sure the designers were doing the best they could just as I had done with the sketch on the cover of my fifth-grade report.

I remember the names I had given to the players on the team; Mad Dog, Doctor Death, Pete, and Chablauwski. (There were actually five members on the team but I never named the goalie, as he never came out of the net to celebrate. Poor guy. Doomed to an 8-bit world where he couldn't even leave his post, and me not even bothering to name him. My apologies to thee ole tender of the goal!)

Dr. Death and Mad Dog were the muscle of the team. Pete, who was very poorly named in comparison to his teammates, gave our team the speed it needed, while Chablauwski was my go-to guy. He was the lone shining star in a drab, gray, Czechoslovakian sky.

I remember yelling at the screen, "You're blowing it Chablauwski!" on the rare occasion he made a bad play. Being the star sometimes means that when you don't shine so bright people take notice and then yell at you. That must have been the highlight for the goalie though, since being anonymous also meant that he could not be verbally berated nor discouraged. I hope that thought at least brought him some comfort as he skated up and down in front of that cold and empty net, time and time again.

However, I now have been through two of the three mental reference materials listed in my internal card catalog and once again there was no useful working knowledge of the country of Czechoslovakia. That is of course, unless I run into a man named Chablauwski who is doing something wrong, in which case I can inform him quite emphatically that he is, in fact, "blowing it."

Strike two.

It was the bottom of the ninth and the mighty Casey was up to bat. Item three read as follows: "Cap'n Crunch with Crunch Berries is by far the superior cereal within the Cap'n Crunch line."

What the hell?

Oh, things were not looking good in Mudville. It appeared that the Mighty Casey had yet again gone down swinging like a once great prizefighter coming out of retirement. His sweaty face hitting the mat with a sickening thud and its echo would shatter all his previous victories. Though a useful tidbit of knowledge and absolute cereal truth, Cap'n Crunch would prove to have nothing to do with Czechoslovakia; I had apparently misfiled this one. Either that or my Dewey Decimal System was severely out of whack. I blame it all on Mrs. Allard. She was our school secretary, who also doubled as our school librarian. It was her job to teach us how to use the card catalog in the first place.

Instead all that she taught me was to harbor an irrational fear of returning books late because then you had to pay her a penalty of fifty cents. (Seriously, you would have to pay her fifty friggin cents. Even though the book was in the classroom right next to the library and you could easily walk there and get it, she would make you pay her fifty cents. If you didn't have the book with you again on the next library day, the fee went up. I never understood it, the book was always right next door. Why couldn't we just go get it if it was so imperative the book is returned? I wonder what she did with the money? Maybe she kept it in a jar and when she retired went on a cruise, sailing the musty seas of late fees.)

So, with very limited knowledge of the land, I bravely took to the streets of Slovakia. My only hope was that someone asked me about Cap'n Crunch or needed me to return a library book for them in a prompt fashion.

First impressions usually are quite indicative of what is to follow in all aspects of life. Be it in dating, visiting a new country, or the first bite of a greasy grilled cheese, pretty much that first taste will predict the aftertaste. My first taste of Slovakia was to be no exception.

I was initially quite taken with the sharp contrasts of the town called Piestany. A stellar example of opposites, of constants in a changing world, of what can happen when you don't speak the native language and have a working knowledge of the land based on construction paper, video games, and misappropriated breakfast cereals. The surrounding buildings and architecture were very old and most likely harkened back to the days of Communist rule. When Mother Russia was still nursing her suckling children from her large, cold, iron teat. When the Czech Republic and Slovakia joined forces to form Czechoslovakia.

Dark statues loomed like shadows across the landscape guarding the secrets of yesterday and the hopes for a brighter tomorrow. Most of the buildings are still very drab and colorless. Maybe this is why I had instinctively gone with the gray construction paper as a child. Perhaps even when I was only a boy who had just shed his bowl cut, I had some psychic foreshadowing of the man I would be in my thirties. Too bad I never did anything of purpose that could have proven to be useful. Instead, I ate cereal and played video games.

In stark contrast to some of the gloomy exteriors, lining the cityscape and filling the flowerboxes were some of the most beautifully vivid roses and poppies that I have ever seen. In one instance, I witnessed a single red poppy growing betwixt the cracks of cold and gray masonry; a sprig of life jutting out of certain death; an elderly man with a raging hard on.

I was briefly reminded of my hotel room (because of the stark contrast, not the morning wood), where I had the world's coarsest toilet paper and yet the softest pillow ever made. It cradled your head like your fat aunt's bosom during the annual, unavoidable, Christmas hug, while the toilet paper literally tore you a new one.

As far as the roses dancing in the flowerboxes go, I am no botanist. I cannot tell you what exact type they were or anything like that. As a matter of fact, the only reason I even knew that the non-roses were poppies was because of that scene in *The Wizard of Oz* where Judy Garland falls asleep in the poppy field.

Side note on Judy Garland: though fetching in *The Wizard of Oz*, I think Miss Garland was especially ravishing in *Meet Me in St. Louis*. I still fancy the Trolley Song. "Zing, zing, zing, went my heartstrings," indeed. I recall that I had to watch that movie as a part of my Film Studies course whilst a student at Rhode Island College. (It was the only class I would go in for. I spent most of my time eating candy cigarettes and playing a Rocky and Bullwinkle pinball machine. I left that school the day of the O.J. Simpson verdict after spending all my money in the pinball machine. "Clang, clang, clang, went the bell.")

I remember sitting in the darkened classroom watching Judy sing while on the trolley car and thinking, "Damn, she was hot." Then I pondered what that might have meant as to being a comment on my sexuality, as I know she still has a very adoring community of gay men. So, I awoke my good friend Rich Fredette, otherwise known as Mr. French, who was sleeping on the desktop next to me. (He slept the entire semester. Like a parakeet, he would go to sleep as soon as someone put a towel over his cage and the world became dark, but he still managed to pass the course. That simple fact coupled with his unbelievable luck at blackjack only goes to prove that God loves a Frenchman.) Mr. French assured me that she was indeed hot and that neither of us was gay. He then returned to his slumber and I to my movie. I always wondered what happened to his mid-class naps after I left that school, as he had no one to wake him when class was over.

Meanwhile back in Oz, or in my case Slovakia, much like my friend with the jewel encrusted bath slippers, I too was far away from home. This was the first place I had ever traveled to where it became apparent that not everyone knew a little bit of English. Regardless, I figured all would be well. Language barriers I could deal with, just as long as there were no winged monkeys flying about.

Most of the food menus had an English translation, though some of them were not exactly phrased correctly, which made for funny light reading. One menu proudly proclaimed its' speedy take-out service with the phrase, "Order for the take home with the fasty." Brilliant. I love anything with the "fasty".

Restaurants proved not to be a problem, as the friendly wait staff would allow me to point like a child at things I thought looked appetizing. Plus, most of the waiters and waitresses knew enough English to walk you through the ordering and bill paying process.

Feeling confident in my verbal skills I thought I would try some things out on the locals. I have always considered myself to be a friendly fellow and thus I try to greet everyone with a smile and a "Hello," unless I am feeling like a particularly fancy boy during which times I might use a hearty, "Good day," as my greeting of choice.

Now I cannot be sure if it was just a cultural difference or a linguistics thing, but not one person on the street during the entire week I spent in Slovakia returned my greeting or friendly smile, though they did hold an uneasy gaze. I even went as far as to learn the Slovakian greeting to try and bridge the gap, but to no avail.

So, by the end of the week I decided to have a little fun with it. Instead of "Hello," my morning walk salutation was "Turtle," which was met with the same non-response.

There was however, one exception.

A delightfully colorful fellow with a broad smile and a mustache was bounding down the street. I abandoned my custom salutation of "Turtle" and randomly said "Piggy-Piggy" to Mr. Mustache. To my surprise and delight he kindly replied "Piggy-Piggy" with a nod of his jolly bobble-head. Finally, I had made contact! I had a friend in Slovakia.

Though I never saw Mr. Mustache again, during my morning walks I had observed a very large amount of older men and women going about with crutches and canes of all sorts. Legs were wrapped with bandages and splints were on wrists and arms. It turned out that the town of Piestany was built atop a natural spring and thus attracts a lot of elderly visitors whom come to the spa for relaxation and rehabilitation.

One morning, whilst enjoying the free hotel breakfast and listening to Copa Cabana by Barry Manilow, I looked up from my smiley face that I had made with my egg yolks and bacon, only to see that the entire cafeteria was filled with little white haired men and women wrapped in vibrant white robes. For a second I thought I was dead. Perhaps I choked on my bacon and this was the welcoming committee for Heaven, whom I just happened to catch at breakfast. I found it odd that they would choose to receive me with Manilow playing in the background, but it was pleasant nonetheless.

This was a very odd sight to start the day with. They looked like some bizarre old age cult ready to board the spaceship to take them to a retirement home on Venus.

Suddenly flashes of the 1980s movie *Cocoon* flashed in my head. I was hoping to find Wilford Brimley somewhere in the crowd. I have always found his soft tones comforting and his walrus like mustache amusing. Wilford Brimley was the one man who could make oatmeal seem like fun. The memory of his golden voice calling out "It's the right thing to do, and the tasty way to do it" still makes me want to heat up a bowl of oats and dive right in.

I always thought Mr. Brimley would make the world's best mall Santa. I can almost hear his inviting "Ho-Ho-Ho" echoing in my made-up childhood.

I wish I could call him up and have him read me a rousing rendition of Good Night Moon at bedtime. How sweet my dreams would be! Filled with a sticky sea of oatmeal, youthful aliens, and a variety of government issued pamphlets on how I can get my diabetes medication and free glucose meter.

Dang, I had just seen him doing those diabetes commercials recently; in hindsight, I should have kept an eye out for him at the juice bar, or at the very least checked the pool for him. Oh well Wilford, we will always have our morning bowls of hot oatmeal on cold winter mornings.

At the end of it all, I found Piestany to be a charming little town, even if I couldn't communicate with everyone. And even if I did they probably wouldn't show me where Mr. Brimley was hiding anyway.

I would certainly have to make a better record of Slovakia in my mind now that I have walked its streets and experienced a sliver of Slovakian life. I approached my mental card catalog, returned the aforementioned reference materials and made the appropriate updates in regards to the scenery, the food, the people, and my personal favorite, Mr. Mustache voicing the words "Piggy Piggy."

Somewhere out there Mrs. Allard would be proud that I was still using the card catalog, filing things appropriately, and returning my reference materials in a timely fashion.

She would also be out fifty cents.

The Cleany and I

During my travels, I was lucky enough to stay in the homeland of my ancestors and that of so many others, Italy. I was in the town of Trieste to be exact. Just over the Slovenian border, in the northeast of Italia.

The sleepy little harbor town does a fair business of food, wine, and gelato along with quaint Italian made clothing shops and such.

My hotel was called The Jolly Hotel, despite the surly personality of the underground parking attendant, whom I really couldn't blame since his job entails him sitting underground all day inhaling exhaust fumes. Why do you think those trolls who dwelt beneath bridges in those fairy tales were so irritable? The Jolly Hotel was good, as far as hotels go. It was clean and had air conditioning, soft towels, internet access, and one of the best free breakfast buffets that I have ever bellied up to.

It has been my experience, that outside of these basic necessities, anything else a hotel can offer you is purely superfluous. The Jacuzzis and swimming pools quickly lost their luster after someone explained to me the process by which people lose skin cells and pubic hair; in particular, the effects of natural suction created by elderly women swimming laps and utilizing the frog stroke.

One problem that I have encountered in hotels all around the world is that of maid service. It is in my personal opinion that no one should clean up after you unless you are an infant or you are elderly; pretty much anyone wearing a diaper, it is okay to clean up after. Being lost somewhere in the desert that is the middle of my life, far from my sunrise and hopefully from my sunset, I currently do not require anyone's assistance in making my bed or wiping my bottom.

Now, in most cases, every hotel room comes complete with a few things:
- Smurf sized bars of soap
- A shot glass of shampoo
- Moisturizing cream, which, let's face it, most people use for, ummm, "personal lubricant"
- Oversized towels to dry your bottom
- A mini bar to dull the pain
- The customary Do Not Disturb sign

However, when you are in Europe, not all the hotels have these things. The Jolly Hotel in Trieste, Italy, did not have a Do Not Disturb sign.

I have run into this problem before, so I have borrowed, well, okay, I stole, a Do Not Disturb sign from a hotel in England. It is a purple-maroonish color with sheep on it, and cleverly enough it reads, "Please do not disturb. I am counting sheep." It works well since it clearly conveys the meaning of the sign with its illustration even if the person reading it cannot read English, or cannot read at all. This sign has come in handy at a few places and has granted me the luxury of some extra beauty sleep in addition to alleviating the fear that the maids are going through my bags, taking my electronics or putting my toothbrush in unspeakable places.

Seriously, how many poop stained toilets, secretion filled sheets, and puke stained carpets would you have to clean before quietly taking your revenge? Due to these thoughts and my extreme paranoia of toothbrush defiling, I take no chances and keep everyone out of my room at all times. So, with confidence in my little purple-maroonish plastic sign, I hung it upon the doorknob like a child hangs his Christmas stocking, with care. I have grown very fond of my little sheep and the sleep and security with which they have provided me over the many months on the road.

I do not condone stealing, as it is against the commandments and I would not want to spit in the face of Jesus like the Roman soldiers did so many years ago. I think you would agree, regardless of your spiritual party affiliation, that we should not take what is not ours. Whether it is money, electronics, husbands, wives, or little plastic door hangers, if it is not yours then you shouldn't take it.

As I laid my head down to sleep and gently closed my eyes, I had silently prayed that things like little plastic door knob hangers did not rank up there with the sins of adulterers and pedophiles. I would not want to spend an eternity in Satan's sauna clinking beer bottles with Hitler just because I desired a little extra sleep and felt the need to defend the integrity of my toothbrush. All in all I thought I would be okay, and thus slipped silently aboard the last train to Slumberville; the click-clacking of the tracks singing a hobo's lullaby for this weary traveler.

Somewhere in between dreams of eating grilled cheese and mentally altered visions of Sesame Street featuring me as Super Grover, I awoke with a startle.

Two quick side notes that will give you an understanding of how such dreams can be possible. First off, yes, I actually do very often dream of food, and even more often I dream of my favorite childhood television programs featuring me as a character. I like to think that maybe whilst the adult me is sleeping, the little kid in me still lives on during the night. Sneaking around the corners of my gray landscape mind while I slumber, indulging in all sorts of things that truly keep my inner self a happy little bastard. Secondly, as it pertains to Muppets, puppets, and the hierarchy of Sesame Street, I have always felt a kindred spirit within the seemingly empty eyes of Grover. Though I will defend to the end the Cookie Monster's right to be himself and eat cookies as his daily sustenance rather than vegetables, no matter how many lazy kids out there in TV land get chunky, he should not have to change his eating habits. It is against his very nature, not to mention his telltale moniker. Many times, while cornered in a frightful reality full of vulgarity, gift-wrapped in deception, I find myself comforted by humming a few bars of, "C is for Cookie and that's good enough for me."

The Count was also a personal favorite as I enjoyed his choice to live a life of solitude in a stormy castle while merely counting objects around the house and no doubt, the days of his life away. Anyhow- my apologies for the derailment, back to the Muppet at hand, Grover. Grover was always my main man—err ... puppet? Not only was he cuddly and loveable and self-promoting of both facts, but also, he held down a day job and I respect that. You would be hard pressed to remember any of the main characters on Sesame Street holding down a job besides Grover. He quietly slaved away as a waiter, bringing soup to very ungrateful customers time and time again, while deep inside harboring his dream of being a super hero. I applaud him, his efforts, and his commitment to overplay the hand that he was dealt, or in his case, had shoved firmly up his furry blue butt. And now back to the lecture at hand, which is not shoved up anywhere- thankfully.

Out of a sound sleep a foreign speaking maid who apparently had no respect for my little plastic door hanger slapped me back to reality. Either that or she was excited by the possibility that the little plastic door hanger meant that there were sheep inside the room, and she secretly shepherded some strange type of wool fetish.

Either way, I was not amused and I was under clothed. I rolled onto my side and made my best attempt at communication. There were two things working against me; my vocal chords need a few minutes to warm-up when first I awake, and secondly, I do not speak Italian.

To be honest, I do not think she spoke Italian either. It has been my experience that wherever you travel, the maids are always from some other foreign land. I imagine there must be some sort of foreign exchange maid program that the hotels participate in. I am not sure what the benefit would be; I suppose it's just to keep up appearances as people have come to expect their maid to not speak the native language.

As she opened the door my groggy appearance, coupled with my zombie like attempts at speech were enough to deter her. She put up her hands in an apologetic fashion, mumbled something about "cleany" and was on her merry way.

With the uniformed threat thwarted and my toothbrush safe by the sink, I returned to sleepy land.

I fell back into my bed and was just about back into my REM cycle, by which I mean Rapid Eye Movement and not anything to do with the 80s band of the same name, when once again I heard the plastic key slide into the door, the hinges creak, and the soft footsteps of my would-be toothbrush assailant.

Still smelling of sleep, I rolled out of bed once again and made my way to the oblivious maid. She was startled by my approach in the darkened room and again she showed me the palms of her hands in an unspoken apology, and she stepped to the door. I pointed to my little plastic door hangar and saw her eyeball the sheep defiantly. She tersely said, "No cleany?" in a questioning yet accusatory tone, to which I shook my head and said, "No. No cleany."

The following three days at the Jolly Hotel were a blurred merry-go-round of the maid crossing my doorstep and I sending her on her way with a polite, "No cleany."

On the fourth morning I tried my best to convey my wishes to the front desk staff. There I found a stocky man in a wrinkled shirt that seemed to understand that I did not want to have my room serviced. I felt encouraged by his warm smile; like melted mozzarella my worry of room intrusion simply slipped away. I decided it was best I relax and so I went on a most enjoyable day trip to Venice, assured that my toothbrush would be safe from the intrusive cleany.

Unfortunately, like cold and congealed mozzarella my lunch came back up on me while returning to the Jolly Hotel. My room was suddenly unfamiliar. Fresh folded towels were on the rack and the pile of dirty towels was strangely absent. The bed sheets were tucked in so tightly that I dare call them virgin.

I was a victim … of the cleany.

I checked my backpack; iPod, camera, video camera, all still there. I looked to the desk in the corner; my laptop was still sitting there with good posture, proudly piping out Cab Calloway's "Poppa's in Bed with His Britches On".

I felt okay, a little violated but okay. Then it happened.

I looked through the doorway into the bathroom.

There it was.

My toothbrush.

Did I leave it on the counter or did I put it upright in the glass?

I thought I had placed it in the holder alongside the sink like I normally do.

Noooooooooooo! Damn you cleany!

Budapest City Limits

Whilst traveling across Eastern Europe I had the opportunity to spend one night in the city of Budapest, which is in the heart of Hungary. The city itself is divided by the mighty Danube River, which I have heard mentioned many times before, but damned if I knew where it was or of what historical significance it may have held. Nonetheless, there it was and so was I; it was good to take note of anyhow as it would probably be the only time the two of us would be sharing a taxi across the universe.

I'm a man who enjoys long walks and letting the cool nighttime air fill his head. I harbor an extreme weakness for ice cream, despite its unflattering effects on my waistline. I also enjoy sipping an ice-cold lemonade while the soothing tones of Louis Armstrong dance and play across my soul; but since this is a story about Budapest and not an online dating profile, I shall digress about what it is that makes me a happy boy and stick to the facts as they pertain to this writing.

As you may well know, due to its recent notation, I am a man who enjoys long walks and letting the cool nighttime air fill his head. And so, as the sun swung low over a weathered landscape like an old man's testicles in flannel pajamas, I decided to take an aimless wander throughout the city streets to see what sights were offered for a man whose heart still pumps wanderlust.

There were many beautifully designed bridges that crossed over the Danube like veins across the back of an elderly woman's hand. Gold plated buildings that reminded me of the Taj Mahal, or at least of some seedy Vegas strip casino, glimmered like a mirage across the cool, rippled surface of the dark waters.

Gelato stands were on the corner of almost every block, which were quite tempting as they glittered and made my belly rumble like a Thursday morning garbage truck as it chugged slowly down Hunger Lane amongst the rubble of what was yesterday's fancy.

A rickety yellow trolley crawled through the city; a crooked caterpillar slinking around the homeless people as they were rearranging their boxes for yet another disappointing night in a long string of disappointing nights.

As my eyes sucked up the scenery and gathered images for a mental scrapbook I would never find the time to make, it was becoming apparent to me that after you have been in one major city, it is safe to say you have been in them all. Sure, the languages may be foreign, the skin tones a different hue than in the previous metropolis; but mathematically speaking, which I do very rarely as I am not fond of numbers and find them untrustworthy, there is a common denominator amongst humanity.

This great equalizer can usually be found after the businessmen and women have driven their Mercedes and fancy town cars back home to the nice neighborhoods. After the food vendors have packed up their carts and went out to dinner. After the city shuts her sleepy eyes and waits for Mister Sun to wake her boney behind up in the morning for work.

It is only after these events systematically take place that the floor is yielded to the nightwalkers, to those who society shuns during the daylight. The ones swept under the rug. The toys stuffed in a child's closet, the porn mag hidden under the mattress when Mom and Dad come to check the room; these are things that make us all human, dirty and equal; yesterday's beautiful and unique snowflakes discarded amongst the prom dresses and dried up Christmas trees.

The great common denominators, in the great bedroom of the world, are the poor, the destitute, and the prostitutes. Women of the night, call girls, escorts, lot lizards, whores, tricks, hookers; these ladies are part of the dirty foundation of our very own society's economy.

As soon as man found shiny rocks in a cave he started trading them to women for sexual niceties, and thus it began.

And now in our super-sophisticated, highly-civilized, modern-day world, when it's sleepy time, these women, men, and men masquerading as women, take their rightful throne as the people who really know how to make the globe keep on spinning; for a price, of course.

I have seen them in countless places across North America, South America, Mexico, Canada, Romania, New Zealand, Africa, and Asia, just to name a few. I have even seen them amongst the elite fog-breathers of Jolly Ole' England; what do you think it is that keeps them so jolly after all? I can assure you it is not the exquisite choice of cuisine.

Come to think of it I have seen prostitutes reclaim the night almost everywhere except for Ireland. Ah, the luck of the Irish, I suppose. At night, their land becomes an enchanted wonderland of fairies and the wee folk as opposed to the drag queens and trick turning ladies of other not so magical lands.

High above Hungary the stars were popping on like streetlights in the heavens and so I made a turn back towards my hotel, snuggled betwixt the dirty pillows of Buda and Pest. Mom always told me to come home when the streetlights came on and maybe she was on to something as I noticed just how much the landscape had changed with the rise of the moon.

The streets themselves went from a calming stonewashed gray to a slick and seductive black; from an innocent baptismal gown destined for salvation to a slinky cocktail dress destined for a hotel room floor. And the orange city lights that once pierced the night like a hymen on a honeymoon, now offered only the briefest flicker of hope.

People flowed out of alleyways and doorways flooding the streets with a sea of flesh and used syringes. For many runaway daughters with daddy issues, prostitution and drug use are as perplexing a question as the chicken and the egg. Did one exist because of the other? Which one came first? Which one came next?

The world's oldest profession hanging on the arm of its dirtiest little secret, together they made for a twisted child only a mother could love.

I had only made it a few paces when a smarmy gentleman whom I would describe as well-worn suede, slinked towards me and gestured excitedly to a building behind him while speaking in a foreign tongue.

Since I am neither a cunning linguist nor a rocket scientist, I was happy this gentleman's offer was not a very complicated one. It took just the briefest of moments to realize what was in store for a nighttime tourist in the city of Budapest, and just in case I needed confirmation he said the one word I have never appreciated for the upper parts of a woman's anatomy: "Tits."

I personally have always felt rather like a boob for the few times I have ever used the aforementioned "T" word, and so I now rank it right up there with the universally dreaded "C" word: colonoscopy. But my irrational fear of words aside, the city of Budapest was about to slip into something a little more comfortable.

Buildings I had just passed with darkened windows now sprang to life like a limp old penis on a certain blue pill. Pimps walked from corner to corner checking in on their merchandise. For as far as the eye could see, the street was now lined with neon signs offering

"Peep Shows," "Cabarets" and the simply stated "Naked Girls".

Now, I never said I was running for sainthood. I'm not even politicking to be an angel. I am just hoping to score an invite to the after party upstairs; if I get into the V.I.P. room, then so be it. Truth be told, there were many earlier versions of myself that could have been found taking in some of the local sights at center stage; putting some poor girl through college one greasy dollar bill at a time. But as we age we grow, or we are at least supposed to, in theory. I for one am proud to report that, although I have yet to attain enlightenment, I have found redemption.

Being a husband who stays legit has become the high school football trophy I was much too scrawny to ever obtain. I hold on to my wedding vows proudly and keep them near and dear to my heart. I have never been one of those guys who say, "What happens in Vegas stays in Vegas." Besides, even if it happened in Vegas, venereal diseases are forever for they know not the city limits.

And so, as a good little soldier for Christ, I shrugged off the stealthy advances of numerous flesh peddlers, pointed the bow of my earthly vessel towards salvation and set my course for the safety of the hotel, hoping to stay one step ahead of loneliness and two steps ahead of the Devil; though he has been known to catch up fast.

Whilst traveling, I am at least comforted in the knowledge that I am only away on business, and barring some horrific fiery plane crash or messy water landing, odds are good that I will make it home once again. I cannot imagine what it must be like for those in the military for whom tomorrow may never come; and for whom I have much respect. But all tomorrows aside, being on the road, far from home and the ones that you love is by far one of the toughest things that any one would ever have to do.

Thoughts of your hometown and your loved ones can play over and over in your mind like a flickering drive-in movie that you are no longer a part of. You sit there heartbroken, homesick, lovelorn and lonely, knowing all the while that the final credits of your life are slowly crawling nearer and nearer the top of the screen at that very moment.

Soon the usher, perhaps in a red vest with a sweeping broom, perhaps in red flesh with a pitch fork, perhaps in his throwback black robe and sickle, or maybe in the guise of John Lennon with an ice cream cone (depending on which theater you patronize and which god or goddess you may or may not subscribe to), someone will come and inform you that the show, your show, is over.

There will be no encore.

To fight off the craziness that is pinning reality's shoulders to the mat, you will start to remember the good times you have spent with your friends and family. To starve off the lonesomeness you will start to imagine the things that you will do with the ones you love when you triumphantly return home again like the mighty Caesar to Rome. And it works … for a little while.

Eventually this type of mental masturbation drives you insane, even if your endowment is more than substantial it can never stretch across the oceans, across the many miles and too distant smiles in your mind; thus, leaving you frustrated, empty and alone. The term "suspended animation" comes to mind, it is not the right word, but you get the point.

It feels as if your real life is paused somewhere on God's television while he is in the kitchen fixing some butter flavored Jiffy-Pop popcorn and getting a root beer.

It's during these times that I too seek a release; something to make everything seem just a little bit more bearable. A little reward for myself as it was; a sweet escape from the loneliness and the impending insanity; a smiley face sticker on my homework that truly was not deserving of one.

As I shuffled with my head down low and my spirits even lower, I was gaining on the next corner when, as the Beatles would say, "I saw her standing there." She was cocoa colored with a creamy complexion, temptingly sweet, and one hell of delicious figure; two healthy scoops on top with a tight and sweet bottom.

If Jiminy Cricket was supposed to be on my shoulder coaxing me into the right decisions, he must have had a sore throat or called in sick because I didn't hear any words of discouragement being whispered in my ear.

And so, with my tongue hanging out like the chunky kid at an all you can eat Chinese buffet, I excitedly hurried over to the gentleman on the corner to negotiate the price. The adult in me told me not to, but the piggy in me could hardly wait to enjoy her, to hold her softly against my lips and explore her sweet sinful beauty; to give into temptation and let go of the conscious burden. To make the wrong decisions and let the chips fall where they may.

Under the dirty glow of Budapest electricity, cash was exchanged. With a flick of his wrist the merchant unceremoniously handed her over to me; the deed was done, she was mine, all mine.

As I walked back to the hotel, holding her in my hands, I was untouchable. I was King of the castle, master of my own domain, and every other modern day cliché.

I thought to myself, there really is nothing like walking down a sin filled city whilst greedily holding on to your own perverted indulgence: a double-scooped sugar cone of mocha-flavored gelato. Decadent. Delicious. Delightful. The pure innocence of it all contrasted against the alternative soul sullying activities was something to behold, something to be proud of, and something to assuage my guilt for the unnecessary caloric intake. To be above the sexual temptations, to be free of the flesh; perhaps enlightenment isn't as far away as I think.

Sure, my hands may have been sticky with ice cream drippings, but at least my conscience was clean.

Land of Love

Like a stake in the heart of vampire country, I found myself stuck in Romania, or Transylvania to be more specific. Deeply swaddled in thick green forests, the city of Cluj sits like a mini metropolis, a dropped lantern amongst the timbers just waiting to ignite with an accelerant mix of sexed up tension and caged love.

Walking beneath the contrast of modern industrial buildings and the cross-bearing towers of elaborate old world churches, one can find the usual city scenes of people hustling and bustling to work whilst the cool kids smoke their cigarettes on the street corner and the Goth kids lay in the church courtyard staring up at the clouds in either a moment of awe at life's greater mysteries, or in sheer defiance of God's love. You can never truly be sure with Goth kids.

I witnessed wrinkled and leathered gypsy women pedaling their herbs, vegetables, and various goods beneath their multicolored bandanas and a scorching Romanian sun.

Under the cool and forgiving moonlight, I saw younger women who were busy pedaling goods of their own.

I suppose we all have something to sell and something to hide.

It's the great equalizer of life since Jesus went home; none of us have to be perfect anymore, but we are called to try.

During a morning walk I stumbled across one business that was selling something for which the people of Cluj were lining up. It was just a glass window behind which a woman was handing out some type of food. A sign hanging from its wall showed a rudimentary drawing of what I interpreted to be a very irate lump of bread dough.

It stood several inches high and wore a surly expression, as well as green sweatbands upon its wrists, and red sneakers down below. Flames shot from its head, either to show that it was angry, it was hot, or that its spider-sense was tingling. "Gogoasa Infuriata" was written in bold letters above the grimacing gob of goo. I'm far from bilingual, but I quickly deduced that "infuriata" meant something to do with being furious and that "gogoasa" meant, well, something else.

Whatever it meant, I was intrigued. Judging by the line of people, these "gogoasas" must have really been something special to behold, no matter how angry they may be to actually be held.

I fell into line with all the other good little civilian soldiers and awaited my first furious experience. Quickly glancing at the signs in the window I saw words like vanilla, chocolate, and caramel, as well as one called "simple."

It has been my personal experience that you can pretty much never go wrong with chocolate, but to get a good base reading on any confectionary treat you should always start out with the stripped-down model and build from there.

It is all very scientific, I know; I have put a lot of time into this field of study.

Through very bad gesturing, pointing like a monkey, and various acts of poor miming, I was able to communicate to the woman behind the glass exactly what my intentions were. She shook her head in disgust and handed me the "simple" that I had ordered. I politely nodded and thanked her in a language she didn't understand hoping that my good-natured intentions would shine through anyway. She ignored me and quickly moved on the next customer leaving me to wonder if perhaps she was a little "infuriata" herself.

My initial impression of the "gogoasa" was that it was something of a doughboy or funnel cake, like the kind you would buy at an American fair ground while trying to win the heart of a girl in a short skirt and a tight sweater; staring at the shine of her lip-gloss while the lights of the carnival rides danced across the empty ballroom of her eyes, and the music of the night stole your heart away forever. Ah youth.

What followed my first bite of the "gogoasa" was a sugary delight for the sense of taste, which in my opinion has the best job of all the senses. I think the sense of smell received the short end of the stick. How many times do you hear the word "smell" and think it's a good thing?

Fundamentally I suppose the "gogoasa" is closest compared to a jelly donut, but it's bigger, like a small pizza folded in half.

I quickly banged a U-turn and got back in line for more, like a kid who just got off Santa's lap and had forgotten to ask for his Red Ryder B.B. gun with a compass in the stock.

This time I cut to the chase with the woman behind the glass and just pointed excitedly to the sign that said something close to chocolate and once more to the one that said something close to vanilla. I was thinking of holding up the end of my nose to show her that I was a piggy, but I did not want to get my message misconstrued and make her more "infuriata," so instead I once again said "thank you" and nodded, and she once again ignored me.

I was high stepping it down the street with a smile on my face and a song in my heart; my hands covered in a sugary residue, as if I had just given the Pillsbury Doughboy a friendly stroke. Truly these "angry donuts," as I would later find out they were called, were a sweet slice of God's love for us here on earth- regardless of whatever god or goddess you may or may not subscribe to.

I looked around for some Romanian's who were experiencing the same palatal bliss as I, but found none. There were plenty of people eating these things, why was no one happy? Perhaps that's where the "infuriata" came in.

Then suddenly the camera in my mind snap zoomed out to a wide shot, just like in Planet of the Apes when you see the Statue of Liberty's head on the beach, and then it hits you all at once. My realization of course was a bit different as there were no "damn dirty apes" and I was no young Chuck Heston. However, just as shockingly, I saw for the first time that it would appear no one here was happy. How could it be that there were a few thousand people on the streets of Cluj, and not one with a smile on their tanned face?

I had observed a similar phenomenon like this once before, a few countries over in Slovakia. In that case, people just were not returning my smile and greeting, but let's face it, Americans don't have the greatest of reputations in lands abroad.

Here in Romania, it appeared that the good people of Cluj were not even trading smiles amongst each other. I had to be missing something somewhere, and so I did what I always do. I quickly recapped the situation by checking the yellow sticky note I keep in my head for just these occasions.

The note read as follows:

Romania

The town of Cluj is pleasant and clean.

The countryside of Romania is gorgeous and sprawling.

By day you can buy fresh produce and herbs on the street.

By night you can buy, well, something else, probably not so fresh, on the street.

And the best thing of all, they have these incredibly good donuts.

Download more James Brown music.

(All right, so downloading James Brown has nothing to do with

Romania but it somehow was on my note next to a sketch of what I think was a dog wearing a stocking cap. Regardless, James Brown was the hardest working man in show business and his music always makes me want to dance. And I don't mean dance as in swaying back and forth like the lone white boy in an urban club; I mean really working up a sweat, as Mr. Brown would put it, like a "sex machine".)

Everything on the list painted a picturesque landscape the likes of which the world has not seen since the unfortunate passing of everyone's favorite afro sporting, public broadcast television artist Bob Ross.

Romania. What's not to love?

Much like Ebenezer Scrooge's plucky nephew Fred, I decided I would keep my jolly Christmas spirit to the end, even if it meant I ended up buried with a sprig of holly through my heart.

Deep within my mind, somewhere to the left of the pineal gland and to the right of my cartoon archives, I held the belief that perhaps the people of Cluj were keeping up their sour faces as a protective façade for the sticky sweet center that filled them to the seams inside.

Maybe someone had loved them and hurt them before.

Maybe someone had made them a promise by moonlight, only to break it by sunrise.

Maybe, just maybe, they themselves were just like the angry donuts.

I now had a mission, a special purpose, within this foreign land. I would come to understand why it was that the people on the street did not smile. I was on a mission from God. Or at least I was passing the time betwixt angry donuts.

So, with my dark shades on, I looked high, I looked low, and I even looked in a copy of Oh the Places You'll Go. But even the good Doctor Seuss would have been hard pressed to return the joy to this Whoville.

(Side Note: The crazy hairstyles of the Who women as depicted in the Dr. Seuss books, cartoons, and feature films, I have always found to be strangely but specifically erotic, and thus I have taken to call it the hairstyle of the "Who Hottie." But that's just me and I have problems. Carry on.)

All around the town of Cluj I looked, I peeped, and I looked some more. I kept my eyes wide till my peepers were sore. But none could be found. None were around. The only smiles I saw were turned upside down.

Could this be?

Could it really be so?

On the streets, you can buy fruits by day, and by night you can buy a ... ohhh, there it is!

Like the many currently holding their numbered ticket in hand and waiting to be served by Saint Peter himself at the great Jewish delicatessen and bagel shop in the sky, my faith and patience were finally rewarded.

While walking by Bank Transylvania, which is a financial institution despite it being the most ironic name for a blood bank that I could have ever thought of, I finally saw a single smile.

It happened quickly. Just out of the corner of my eye, beyond the images of childhood innocence that I keep stored there for quick reference, I spotted a glistening smile that reflected the hot Romanian sun like a fun house mirror, bright and yet somehow out of place.

Attached to the smile was a nondescript woman who must have become unaware of her surroundings whilst chatting on her cell phone, for once she glanced up and saw her whereabouts she promptly removed her smile, folded it up and placed it in her front pocket along with her phone.

But it was too late, for the Mona Lisa had cracked up at last. There was a momentary break in the darkness to which I was a rare audience member. I thought that this must have been how Ronald Reagan felt when the mighty Berlin wall was brought tumbling down like the world's most famous omelet, Humpty Dumpty.

Ronnie, Ronnie, President of the States- what a great man. I allowed myself adequate pause to recall a mental montage of the 1980's, as I knew them.

It was set to the tune of "Eye of the Tiger" and played out across the drive-in screen behind my eyes like the opening to a family oriented situational comedy.

There was the Rubik's Cube, Pac-Man, Atari, brightly colored spandex, big black sunglasses, acid washed jeans, glam rock, Alex P. Keaton as portrayed by Michael J. Fox on *Family Ties*, Reaganomics, that scene in the movie *Goonies* where Mikey steals his first kiss from the older girl in the dark cave, and then Chunk eats Rocky Road ice cream with the loveable yet grotesque character Sloth, and in the end, everyone got what they needed and they were happy.

The 1980s were a great time, and Hollywood actor turned politician, Ronald Reagan, accompanied by his co-star Bonzo the Chimp, presided over it all like the King of Cartoons. Then the 1990s came about and we all smelled like teen spirit; which, if judging by most the kids in my school was any sort of litmus test, teen spirit smelled a lot like Calvin Klein's less notable scent, "Depression".

There I was, finally in high school and eager to take my slice of pie from the "Me Generation" buffet that the 80s had promised. Fast cars, hot chicks, wild parties, and lots of sexual innuendo, that's what I signed up for. Let's do it!

Alas I was too late, as flannel-shirt gurus from Seattle closed down the happiness buffet for good. The new administration was ushered in, consisting of grunge rock, Bill Clinton, and stained blue dresses. My world as I knew it would never ever be the same.

Clothed in second hand Salvation Army garb, my generation raged against the machine in possibly the most lackadaisical way we knew how, complete and total apathy. If the teenagers from the 60s took a bad trip in their flower powered buses of the 70s and suddenly ran out of gas in the 90s, they would have slapped us all.

I'm not sure if it was the years of Attention Deficit Disorder medication finally taking effect or what, but it would have appeared to the untrained eye of adults, and worst of all teachers, that getting us to feel anything more than the occasional passing depression, was damn near impossible.

The only time we could truly be ourselves was strictly within the company of other miserable bastards who really had no reason to be upset. These were usually events like raves, concerts, and the occasional coffee house- this is where happiness was.

That's when it hit me; perhaps the people of Cluj would only let their guard down when solely amongst their own. They probably weren't too interested in smiling back at large groups of loud Americans. Heck, half the time I wasn't too interested in it either but it had become customary where I came from. Smile on the outside, cry on the inside.

If I were to gain viewing access to the inner workings of the people of Cluj, I would have to do it stealthily and through a very darkened window.

After very little consideration, which is typical for me, as I don't really think most things through, I decided a movie theater might be my best vantage point from which to observe the subject matter at hand.

Funny thing about Romanian movie theaters, or this one at the very least, there was no popcorn. As a matter of fact, there was very little besides a variety of curiously flavored potato chips.

So, there I sat, an American in a Romanian movie theater, watching an American movie, subtitled in Romanian, while the locals sat unaware, noisily crunching and munching their various potato chips.

Suddenly, from beyond the rustling bags and crunching spuds came roaring laughter. It was as if someone cranked up the laugh track to a struggling sitcom. Whether they really found the movie that amusing, or they just like to laugh at bad American movies, had yet to be determined. The only conclusive evidence I could gather was that the daily emotions that sat repressed and tethered, did lie beneath a very shallow surface. A quick glance around the noisy theater showed aisle upon aisle of smiling faces; big grins from ear to Romanian ear.

I stayed to observe for a bit more and was pleasantly rewarded. It was good to hear the laughter and bathe in the good vibes for lately I was becoming more aware of my solitude.

Before the credits had rolled I slipped out into the shadows of the night, careful not to disturb the environment in which I was an intruder. The last thing I wanted to do was disrupt the volcanic eruption of emotion; like a child caught with his pants down mid-stroke the first and only time his parents forgot to knock before entering his pubescent fantasy camp.

Beneath an elegant moonlight that slinked over the streets of Cluj like illuminated fine lace, the Romanians were in love. I watched as they walked hand in hand down the alleyways and along the sidewalks. I longed for the gentle touch of my own wife's hand in mine. I continued to observe the Romanian lovers all the way back to my lonely hotel room.

They kissed at the bus stop.

They kissed at the gas pump.

I'm sure they kissed in private, while doing the humpity hump hump.

Like a disappointed child staring into his cloudy bowl of not so entertaining

Sea-Monkeys, I had finally seen the reality of the situation.

It was not the people of Cluj that were sad and lonely, it was I.

It wasn't that they were closely guarding their emotions. They were just saving them for sincere moments when surrounded with the people in their lives that mattered most, their families and their friends. Or maybe even for a stolen moment shared on a cell phone outside of Bank Transylvania, which really should be a blood bank.

I was the angry donut.

I tried to take comfort in knowing that I would be home soon. I would be home to my lovely wife and our family. Home to popcorn in movie theaters and fake smiling, plastic people on the street.

Alas, somewhere in my mind maybe I already was home; Ronald Reagan was still President, Bonzo the Chimp was flinging his poo, the Romanians were smiling at the people they loved the most, and gogoasa infuriatas paved the streets of Cluj, as well as a bridge back to the States and the ones I love the most.

A Tale of Three Cities

City #1: Sao Paulo

I'm very fond of being an American. I have several pairs of American flag boxers. I watch baseball, football, and lots and lots of NASCAR. I love eating a hot dog right off the grill on the Fourth of July even though it burns the roof of my mouth every time and causes my wife to get that, "God, I married a fool," look.

Come every Halloween, I sit down for a large slice of pumpkin pie with the most generous dollop of whipped cream you ever did see. The chilly autumnal breezes of November bring Thanksgiving, the turkey and all the fixings. At Christmas, the baby Jesus himself would have a hard time prying my lips from the eggnog carton. Seriously, it might get ugly, and I love Jesus, especially baby Christmas Jesus.

I enjoy lots of things about my homeland, but truth be told, I mostly like the food. So, when it came to pass that I should travel to South America, my hopes were that some of our finer cuisine, or at least some of our chain franchises, would have trickled South of the equator; it was an "America" after all, right?

Turns out I was quite wrong. There were some familiar names, but most of them were a far cry from the good ole U.S. of A. So, to distract myself from the constant urge to hop a plane back to the States and make a pig of myself in some roadside greasy spoon I do what I always do, I take a walk.

My first stop in Brazil was the streets of Sao Paulo, which is billed as one of the largest cities in the world. Now, I am much too lazy to research if they mean geographically or population size; plus, with the constant changing facts on Wikipedia, it's hard to get a straight answer, but judging by what my lay before me, it may be based on both.

There were many high-rise buildings for as far as the eye could see, cutting in and out of the yellow tinged smog as it lay above the noisy streets like a dirty blanket that a child just refuses to get rid of. Bumper to bumper traffic stretched the vast landscape and offered not a glimmer of hope to anyone who may have been running late. Busses were packed to standing room only occupancy as if The Beatles were playing and it was 1964.

Feeling lucky to be a pedestrian and only a mere observer of this auto circus, I merrily continued along in my own little world feeling wiser, eco-friendly, and just a little bit horny; though that had nothing to do with the surrounding elements, just rather my usual testosterone V-8 being powered by an over active imagination, lots of sugar, and longing for home.

Motorcycles darted like fireflies around stagnant cars that sat in gridlock fashion; a small army of rusty tortoises. Street vendors yelled in their native tongue what street vendors always yell regardless of their native tongue. The cityscape was carpeted with tables full of bootleg DVDs of the latest Hollywood blockbusters and music compact discs. Others sold newspapers, porno magazines, cheap sunglasses, knock-off watches, jewelry, handbags, and of course remote controls, and calculators. That's right. Just about everything you could—wait a minute—remote controls and calculators? I had to go back and see for myself for I must have been mistaken. Surely, I must have seen just one calculator that the smut peddler uses to add up problem-sized purchases, right?

But there they were; pretty maids all in a row. Calculators. Different sizes, different shapes, and different colors; solar powered, battery powered, and hybrid versions of the two; some with printing tape, but most without. Why in the heck would someone be selling calculators on a street corner? Is doing simple math that much of a problem here in Sao Paulo? Maybe they weren't such a big city after all; the census bureau just did not have the right equipment for the job. I really thought I saw one guy carrying an abacus.

Perhaps they simply harbored an inexplicable love of numbers. My good friend Count von Count, the caped resident of the Sesame Street community (yes, that's his full legal name by the way) he seemed to enjoy himself quite thoroughly with his mental math masturbation, and so why not the people of Sao Paulo?

Satisfied, or at least distracted, with my Muppet math justification for calculator infatuation, I took a closer gander at the remote controls. Some were generic universal style remotes but others were brand specific, and all of them wrapped in plastic wrap like your Aunt Tilly's sofa. And this was not just one eccentric vendor trying to be the cool kid on the block. There were numerous stands in which you could purchase calculators and remote controls. I am sad to report that after several inquiries and investigations, the people of Sao Paulo's love of things with numbers and buttons remains a mystery.

One interesting thing of note did happen on my way out of the city; I was in traffic—surprise, surprise—when a gentleman approached the car selling cell phone chargers, he had a huge handful of them. They dangled and danced in his grasp like a bunch of shiny black snakes. It was at this moment I dubbed Sao Paulo, Brazil's discount flea market of every day electronics; from calculators to phone charges, they certainly have it all.

City #2 Cambuquira

My next Brazilian destination was the sleepy little town of Cambuquira. I call it a sleepy little town because there really isn't much else to do there but sleep. At one time this area was bustling with casinos and boasted some of the finest natural drinking water on earth thanks to the area springs. However, the gambling houses were eventually shut down and apparently no one was staying around for the water, thus the town became quiet and empty, the local people say it has been cursed.

Cursed or not, the tiny little village was nestled into the countryside like a monkey wrench in the backside of a plumber's drawers, comfortable yet sweaty.

The streets were mostly cobblestone and they cascaded up and down the hilly region like a smooth rock waterfall through a sun-faded landscape of what once were vibrant colors.

There were some stores, but not very many. In a small cobble shop, a sad faced shoe man sat playing a weeping guitar to the lonely "soles" that surrounded him. Oh, how I do love puns.

At the town supermarket, you could get whatever you needed, especially if what you needed was soap. They had two and a half aisles lined with different colors, consistencies and sizes; it was like visiting Mister Wonka's factory if Mister Wonka decided to make cleaning products and not candy. As for the locals, I can say that the people of Cambuquira are very clean if nothing else.

Being a wary traveler I made my way back up the crooked hill to my hotel. I was just about to settle in for a long mid-summer night's dream when suddenly there came a tapping, as if someone was gently rapping, rapping outside my chamber---uh, window.

I slipped into my slippers and slid on over to the window, tearing open the sash like in the good ole days. And what to my wondering eyes should appear? But some jabroni riding a motorcycle with a huge subwoofer speaker system strapped to the back. Figuring that every village needs its idiot, I gave it no more than a passing thought and slid back into the shadows of sleepy town.

After exploring the enchanting dreamscape of my twilight memories, I arose from my slumber and gave a nicely exaggerated morning stretch. On my lawnmower of life there is no turtle speed, only rabbit, as I see no sense in doing anything if you aren't going to enjoy it to the maximum level; hence my aversion to regular "stuf" Oreos.

Post exaggerated morning stretch I felt very loose, yet happy, and so I shuffled off to take my Flintstone's chewable vitamin. I was hoping for a red Betty as they are the best and always signify a great day ahead, when suddenly I could feel the floor shake beneath me.

I am no expert on seismic activity and so I had no idea as to whether the "cursed" town was on a fault line; however, I was going to find a doorjamb to hide under and take no chances just in case. This was looking less and less like a red Betty day. The tremors that I felt were accompanied by the gut rattling sounds of over modulated bass frequencies like those I had heard the previous evening, thus proving to be nothing earth shattering.

A quick meander back over to the window proved more exciting than usual. This loud music was not just an American fad catching on fifteen years later, but also a throwback to earlier political strategy. Apparently being Mayor of the "cursed" city was something to strive for. Perhaps if you rose to a certain level of society the curse no longer applies.

There were multiple cars clogging up the roadways like lumps of cholesterol in your superior vena cava. Each vehicle blasting its own outer speaker system while multiple signs complete with polling numbers flapped in the breeze. So, there I stood in my American flag boxer shorts, staring out of my window looking down upon these beat-up cars with their numbers in large print on the doors and roofs, it resembled a very wacky democratic demolition derby arranged just for my own private viewing pleasure. The whole thing left me with a strange sense of nationalism, I felt proud for the sake of democracy itself and, as it would turn out, I was saluting the flag, or at least, part of me was. Perhaps it would be a red Betty day after all.

Ohhhh say can you seeeeeee…

City #3: Rio De Janeiro

When most people hear "Rio" they think of the Carnival festival, the soft sands of Ipanema beach or the nightlife at the Copacabana, the hottest place North of Havana.

The bright nighttime lights of Rio make you almost forget that during the day most of the suburbs look like the ravaged post-apocalyptic cities you see in the movies. Three walled shacks house families who live next to and on top of other families. Their shared walls constructed of two by fours and plywood. The vibrant colors of drying laundry look lost against a defeated and depressed background of misery and poverty.

There are ghettos, barrios, and shanty towns known locally "favelas." In the favelas not even the police are allowed to enter. They are self-sufficient, run by gangs and drug lords. These areas operate independently from Government control. Those who live in them and operate businesses there do not even pay taxes to the Government; instead they pay those who run the area. It is the old-school protection racket at its finest.

High above the sandy beaches, beyond the wild sexy parties, and even escaping the favela bosses, one man stands alone.

High atop Corcovado Mountain, which means "hunchback" in Portuguese, standing 120 feet tall and weighing in at 700 tons, he's turned water into wine, he's raised the dead, he is ... Christ ... the Redeeeeeemer! That's right, the tallest statue of its kind of my Lord and Savior, Jesus Christ, stands there on the mountaintop, His arms outspread, looming over the darkened city like a cross hanging from the neck of a prostitute, dangling over her dirty pillows.

Only eight American dollars for admission, and a bargain at that, will get you full access to the site. A little bus drives you halfway up the mountain from the ticket gate and drops you off at the base of the steps, or as I like to call them, the stairway to Heaven. Jesus comes complete with four souvenir shops, one fancy restaurant, and a snack bar because you should never meet the Lord on an empty stomach.

The souvenir shops are scattered along the stairway so you will see them on both your way up in hopes of getting something to be autographed, and your way down for token mementos and keepsake reminders. There were plenty of rosary beads, wooden plaques, and other typical religious memorabilia. I looked for a giant foam finger that said "Jesus #1," but they must have been sold out. They did have plenty of glow-in-the-dark Jesus statues. And so of course I started singing, "I don't care if it rains or freezes, as long as I got my plastic Jesus." It is a great little song, after all.

Finally, after buying two hotdogs that were sacri-delicious, some rosary beads, and a small wooden statue, I made my way up to the Big Man himself.

I was expecting a line of some sort, like there is for Santa or the Easter Bunny, but there wasn't. There was plenty of room for everyone up at the feet of Jesus and the view was amazing.

Not so much the city that surrounded him, though it was very nice, but to stand at the feet of such a statue, dedicated to someone so important in my own life, and to feel so in awe, it was truly remarkable. I would like to think that regardless of whatever god or goddess someone may or may not subscribe to, this experience still is a nice one.

I was expecting to be moved, but not to such a level. I felt so small, not just in front of the statue, but just in my thinking that I am one man, in such a large world, and even larger universe. My problems and troubles seemed to melt away. I said some prayers for my parents, my wife, our family, and especially my daughter. I was thankful for all that I have been given, and then I prayed for all the people in the city down below and cities just like it everywhere, for all those struggling to get by, for those who are doing what they must do, be it right or wrong, to make ends meet, to provide for themselves and the ones they love. After all, this life is about helping one another, not just oneself.

I am thankful to have found Jesus many years before and not just here on the mountaintop. But it was still a nice reminder, not just of who He is, but who I am, and what this world is all about.

Beep Beep Peru Beep Beep

I find it is always important to learn a little bit about any city you are to be visiting; it was in this spirit that I looked up some things on Lima, the capital city of Peru.

Lima is the 19th most densely populated city in the world, it has a terribly low amount of rainfall, and there is one more thing that has been left out of the history books that I learned firsthand, Lima must be one of the noisiest cities on Earth.

They beep their car horns for pretty much everything, and I mean everything. Light turns green- beep your horn. Light turns red- beep your horn. People in the cross walk- beep your horn. People on the sidewalk- beep your horn. Horn doesn't work- beep your other horn.

And the odd thing about it all is that the people themselves, even while driving and beeping, appear to be in a pleasant mood. Back where I come from, when you beep your horn there is almost always a middle finger or curse word to accompany it. No beep ever travels alone.

But here in the dusty streets of Lima, beeping is part of the atmosphere. I would imagine it sounds like the Road Runner's mating season; should the cartoon bird ever stop and take the time to mate. I wonder if he does everything that fast? I would think that his lover would be quite unsatisfied with his speedy delivery.

Speaking of the desert, (I am aware I never really mentioned the desert, but if you could see inside my animated mind you would see the train of thought which left the station at Lima, stopped by to see the Road Runner and then chugged out through the colorful cartoon sands littered with opened crates from ACME and broken down old coyotes) anyhow, speaking of the desert, because of its incredibly little amount of rainfall, much of Lima is covered with a skim coat of dry, chalky dust. The quaint cobble stone roads in the historic part of the city, the sidewalks of the city center, and all the streets that connect the old to the new are covered with the same tan soot.

I eventually started to pour some of my bottled water on things just to see what their natural colors were. I don't like to waste water, especially not now when our world is in peril thanks to, well, humans, but the alternative was peeing on things as it's the only other way I know how to make my own liquid outside of spitting which I do not fancy. I would suppose that both are disrespectful if not illegal, and so bottled water it was.

There I stood, in the dusty city streets, sprinkling water on this and that, like a demented version of Johnny Appleseed, bringing vibrancy back to the rocks and sculpted marble pieces that dot the city landscape.

I am sure the locals thought I was crazy and maybe they weren't far off, but after days of seeing everything in the same shades of brown I felt the need to bring a little color and breathe a little life into the city.

At the end of my walk I could look back and see exactly where I had been by viewing one shiny surface at a time. There was a vibrant path, sparkling in defiance against its chalky future.

No one passing by seemed to object to my curious behavior; I mean, people were beeping, but what else is new?

Bicycle! Bicycle!

When the members of Queen wrote in their appropriately titled song, Bicycle: "I want to ride my bicycle, I want to ride my bike," they must have been in Denmark. I had only been in Copenhagen for five minutes and already I had seen more people on two wheels than I ever have in my entire lifetime. At first I thought it was some sort of wacky winter bicycle race, but no, this was just people coming and going to work, to the grocery store, to the beauty salon, to buy pornography. It was simply amazing. It was one of those things that I just wasn't expecting to see. It was a moment of clarity, of realization. The American way, where we pretty much drive our gas guzzling SUV's to the store at the end of the street, is not the only way to go.

Personally, I am a walker. I prefer to go on long walks as to any other mode of transportation. Also, I am impossibly bad at roller skating, rollerblading, and skateboarding. And though I am a fair biker, I excel at walking. I mean, okay, admittedly I am clumsy. I walk into things, trip over things, and fall at times, but still, walking is pretty much what I do best, as sad as that may be.

But here before my very eyes were a nation of people who decided that two wheels was the way to go. People wearing suits, people wearing jeans, women in skirts, guys in skirts, kids and the elderly alike, all of them, riding their bicycles. I never would have guessed.

When I thought about Denmark initially, I thought of the great Norsemen. I thought of explorers like Erik the Red, and proof that nepotism isn't something new, his son Leif Erikson. I thought of coo-coo clocks and wooden shoes. I thought of the Swiss Miss Girl and my love for huge mugs of hot chocolate. I thought about the Native American girl on the Land O Lakes butter packaging and how with a little bit of creativity you can fold her knees from the other side of the package backwards, cut a flap on the little stick of butter she is holding and when said flap is lowered, see her boobs. I have issues. I know. I am aware.

I wasn't sure why that's what my mind thought of. Probably because the Swiss Miss girl and the Land O Lakes girl both have long braided hair, and both have to do with my favorite thing- food. Boobs remain a close third. I'm more of a fan of the fanny, which ranks second on my list between food and boobs, which is a great place to be. I bet Erik the Red would agree.

Anyhow, the thought of bicycles and Denmark never crossed my mind. However, it seemed to be all the rage here. Surprisingly I never did see one coo-coo clock or a single pair of wooden shoes, which was probably because it would be a lot harder to pedal a bicycle in a pair of wooden shoes and so I couldn't argue that point either.

The city of Copenhagen was very charming with its brightly colored buildings and gothic statues and architecture. The canals and inlets that dotted the city sidewalks were like that which I have seen nowhere else. Truly beautiful and picturesque; like a postcard that has sprung up to life all around you, immersing you in vivid colors and dreams.

Being a big fan of the Vikings, the explorers and conquerors, not the football team (I'm a Dolphins fan) I became a bit caught up in seeing the dark, icy waters around me, and thinking that these were the same waters that carried these men and women of legend to unexplored territories and back again. Sure, they aren't remembered as the nicest of groups, with all the pillaging and plundering, but you must give them a lot of respect for heading out into unchartered waters in pretty much a large rowboat, often not knowing what they were going to find or if they would ever make it back.

Many, many years and one short airplane ride later, I stand here in Denmark and I am amazed by the mere fact that people choose to ride bikes here. Not quite an exciting discovery in the grand scheme of things. However, in this rapidly evolving world there grows less and less to discover, less and less to explore- unless you can access space or go underwater. (Did I mention I'm not a great swimmer either? So yeah, that's out.) And despite my affection and affinity for astronaut ice cream, there is even less a chance of me getting into space, so, looks like the fact that wooden shoes are a thing of the past, coo-coo clocks have been replaced by digital time pieces, and biking is in- well, that's my grand discovery.

Somewhere Leif Erikson is crying salty tear drops into his mead and his father is simply ashamed of me.

Hitler's Vinter Vunderland

My first mental impression of Sweden was that it was a land of delicious little brown meatballs, cheaply made yet durable office furniture, and of course home to tall, golden giants.

Upon arriving in Sweden I realized that the clear majority of these gold-haired goliaths also had some of the brightest blue eyes that ever gazed upon God's green Earth.

Then I thought of the "Master Race". Then I thought of Hitler. And then I was sad, so I said a prayer and I went to look for some of those little brown meatballs.

Nothing halts the clicking boots of a mustachioed dictator from setting up a hate factory in your heart like filling your stomach with little brown meatballs- if only the Allied Powers knew this earlier.

Unfortunately for me, I am a man of little patience when I am hungry and I can become a bit of an angry dictator myself, and so the quest for little brown meatballs would have to wait until a later time. Hunger Hitler had to be stopped at all costs, so I promptly high-tailed it, rather than goose-stepped it, into the first little pizzeria I saw; God bless the Italians!

Pizza, macaroni, and the Mario Brothers; Italians have once again saved me from hunger, and saved the Princess from whoever she let kidnap her this time.

With my own War on Hunger officially won, my full belly and expanding bladder held a small parade of their own in the nearest public rest facility. Thankfully there was no ticker tape parade or "Mission Accomplished" banner involved, though I do use a fair amount of toilet paper whenever I have the misfortune of having to use a public rest facility. I like to make a nest of sorts.

And so, with three of my four daily necessities checked off the mental "to-do" list as inscribed upon the yellow sticky-note in my cerebellum (the other two being: routine morning hygiene, and watch cartoons), I embarked on a journey to submerge myself in the enchanting land of Sweden.

The landscape itself was quite comforting, dark forests filled with more towering trees than Paul Bunyan and Babe the mighty blue ox could have ever laid waste to. Beautifully sprawling scenic vistas complete with raging rivers, babbling brooks and deep black lakes that were as still as a young man hiding underneath his girlfriend's bed when Daddy unexpectedly came home early from work.

High peaked houses lined the streets; their roofs just capped with snow, recalling the joyously colorful illustrations of childhood Christmas storybooks. The ones with tales wherein Old Saint Nick and his flying reindeer magically tap-danced their way through the sky just above the rooftops of the city below. Children laying in their beds hoping and praying that the big guy just may have had to go to the can and thus missed seeing the time that they shaved the cat.

Strolling through town I couldn't help but admire the amount of candy stores and confectionaries that were around. In America, it is the fast food chains that dimple the walkways of the shopping centers, the superhighways of the nation, and the amply sized bottoms of the public at large. In Sweden, it apparently falls to candy shops to carry that torch.

Being a purveyor of fine sweets and sugary treats (and an admitted Candy Buttons addict), I took it upon myself to sample the gumdrops and candy canes of this veritable winter wonderland.

It only took a couple of bites before sloppy water-colored images of Hansel and Gretel filled my mind, flowing over onto my palate and caressing my taste buds like so many tiny angel kisses. But Hansel and Gretel were German, so it didn't really make much sense and I wondered if my candy was laced with something other than confectionary sugar; but then again, very few things in my mind make much sense at all, and so I assumed all was on the up and up. I blamed it on Hitler and carried on.

I am pleased to report that the only thing sweeter than the candy stores was the Swedish people that ran them. It was as if they would bleed sticky, sweet syrup; though I couldn't find a way to prove that without committing a felony or asking them to donate.

"What's your blood type?"

"Delicious."

Though most the Swedish people physically resemble Adolph's so called "Master Race", they definitely do not resemble his ideals.

Maybe that's why he envied them so?

Maybe he just didn't get enough candy as a kid?

Maybe Santa never brought him any toys?

But then again, he probably wasn't a "good little Hitler" either. The bastard.

The Monsters of Manila

The Islands that make up the Philippines are incredibly breath taking. Winding mountain roads are nestled in some of the most lush and vibrant vegetation that this beautiful world has to offer. As you ascend the twisting and towering peaks it is not uncommon to find a waterfall, a field of sunshine yellow flowers, or royal purple orchids.

Another thing that you are very likely to see, from the busy city streets of Manila to the serene roadways of Baguio City, are the most creatively customized buses that public transportation has to offer.

Standing about five feet high and over eight feet long, these shuttles are more than just a means of getting around; they are fashion statements, religious proclamations, and in some cases, just straight-up shameless self-promotion.

Each one looks like a mini float taking part in a daily nine to five parade, bringing the people of the city to their places of employment and back home again.

Elaborate paint schemes, murals, and the absolute best in chrome, adorn these beasts of the blacktop. Each with a monstrous grille bearing anything and everything from Mercedes emblems to home painted signs declaring the wish for peace, art singing the praises of Jesus as king, or merely a token of affection professing the love of the driver for the queen of his heart, the grille was clearly the crown of these majestic machines.

Within their secure cargo hold, the good people of the Philippines are brought about to do their daily business, twenty or so people at a time. The monster-like buses present a thunderous roar as they rip up the road, bellowing black exhaust that would make Satan himself cough to clear his demonic throat.

Watching the emissions bellow and swirl up through the treetops, one cannot help but wonder exactly how much longer the serene hilltops of the Philippines can stay a pristine environment; how much longer they can shirk off the blanket of smog that already tucks into bed so many large cities across the world.

I am no Vice President and environmental superhero Al Gore, but I assume that the geographical location of the islands, coupled with their dense vegetation must do a little something to help the cause, to aid the Philippine Islands in the war on pollution. It's either that, or the chrome-toothed sneer of the Manila buses as they creep through the blacktopped veins of the Philippines is enough to frighten off the smoky yellow clouds and send them all the way to Los Angeles. Whatever the reason is, the Philippines remains a small hidden treasure tucked away in the Western Pacific Ocean, shrouded in lush scenic vistas and guarded by monsters.

Service With a Smile

While in the Philippines I looked deep inside myself and found out that I was empty- in terms of nutritional sustenance that is. In truth, I was chock full of good moral fiber, and stuffed to the gills with dreams and good will, I just needed a snack.

I surveyed the storefronts of the crowded city streets when my eyes settled upon a truly American type choice, a fast food place called Jollibee.

I am not usually one to eat fast food, but when traveling abroad I have found that nothing makes me feel closer to home than a greasy order of fries and a grilled cheese. Plus, the Jollibee had a statue of its mascot out front, a five-foot smiling bee wearing a chef's hat, a tidy red valet jacket and no pants. That's my kind of bee.

He stands quietly and contently, miming his one simple desire, that you should enter his restaurant and dine upon the feast of the Jollibee; either that or he is just proudly displaying upon his jolly bee face the enlightenment that one can only experience by going sans slacks in the modern world.

Whatever his true motives may have been, who was I to disappoint such a happy fellow? Plus, I am a sucker for a cartoonish mascot; well, pretty much cartoons in general. My mind was made up. "To the Jollibee!" my stomach triumphantly exclaimed.

The appearance of the restaurant interior was not unlike any other fast food franchise whose oil stained floor I have trodden upon countless empty calories before.

Brightly colored plastic booths lined the walls; some crumpled napkins and stray French fries defiled the wood grained tabletops. Somewhere in the back there must have been restrooms thick with the scent of urinal cakes, and of course the usual stray drops of dried yellow that stain the snow-white porcelain bowl brim, for sadly, nothing in this world remains pure, even if the employees maintain it hourly.

After studying the sun-faded menu above the cashier counter I cautiously made my approach like a sweaty palmed child at a grade school dance.

There was a rumble in my tummy and my voice quivered a little as I tried my best to pronounce in a foreign tongue the name of something that resembled a cheeseburger.

With wide eyes and a smile on her face, the young girl under the visor nodded her head emphatically and motioned to see if there was anything else I wanted. I asked if it was possible to get the cheeseburger "without the meat," for I have found that this is the best way to explain the delicious concept of a grilled cheese to fast food clerks in strange lands since it is never on the menu. This also works on McDonald's along the New Jersey turnpike- but sadly it has been my experience that their employees are not nearly as friendly as those at the Jollibee.

The young girl under the visor looked perplexed, but only for a moment when suddenly from behind her popped out the grinning round face of a teenage boy with a striking resemblance to the Cheshire Cat. Seriously- it was like he was hiding behind her the whole time. Curiouser and curiouser.

"Special order sir?" he asked very excitedly.

I nodded in agreement, to which he exclaimed, "Special order! Special order!" as he vanished into the kitchen area, the belly of the bee. Within moments the young man returned, as happy as ever with my "special order."

I thanked them both, promptly paid the wide-eyed girl under the visor, and made my way outside. I ate my delicious melted cheese sandwich under the scorching sun while children canvassed the parking lot for tourists and handouts.

Maybe it's the deep seated Catholic guilt that was instilled in me as a child in parochial school, maybe it's a fragment of an internal constant urge to make up for my past mistakes, or maybe it is just a glimpse of my true inner nature, for whatever the reason may be, the truth of the matter is I have a hard time not giving change to beggars, paupers, and thieves acting as the same. Either way, their lot is the same sorry one, and so I do my best to share what I have been given for I truly believe we are all in this together.

There is a certain mental triage that takes place when I observe a group of people in need, and as in all other aspects of my life, its women and children first. Chivalry isn't dead, at least not as long as I am on the planet.

However, my usual mental checklist presented me with a unique problem that I had never encountered before. I stood within the suddenly judgmental gaze of the once cheerful Jollibee statue, watching with him through his wide staring eyes at a small group of children all doing their best to gain what they could.

I was very sorry to see children dancing, singing, and begging for money as it was, but then to see them turn around and bring it to the shady men whom lurked around the taxi stand like a murder of parasitic crows, well that was something different. It was painful. It was troubling. It was wrong.

I am only one guy visiting for just a few days, and there is short time for me to reverse the Lord of the Flies hierarchy that was evident amongst the children. No doubt this system was put into place by the taxi stand shadow walkers, and no matter how much I wished for the children to stand up for themselves, to struggle, and to be free, I knew that there was not much I could do about it.

So, I did what I could. I walked over amongst the taxi stand men who were giving this one child a particularly hard time. I took all that I had left of their currency out of my pocket and placed it in the outstretched mitten of the little one, the smallest child there; the men looked but didn't move. The larger and older kids were poised to pounce upon him for his newfound wealth. I knelt by the boy and whispered, "Run!" not sure if it would translate, but hoping it would. I figured in this world he was going to grow up fast anyway, I might as well give him hope and something worth fighting for.

The last I saw him he was running as fast as he could—away from the other kids, and to my delight, far, far away from the vultures at the taxi stand who stood there like the cowards they truly were.

The grilled cheese from the Jollibee satisfied my hunger, but seeing that spark of life in that child's eye, it satisfied my soul. And curiously enough, it was just what I ordered, a special order indeed.

Lights Above – Darkness Below

And sometimes you wake up and find yourself in Paris, the City of Lights.

My knowledge of Paris, and pretty much the rest of France, was unfortunately limited to brief images of the Eiffel Tower, the Mona Lisa, and a few animated scenes stored in my mind that were clipped from old *Tom and Jerry* cartoons.

As an American growing up in the 80s, I was raised hearing the stereotypes of the French as a very rude culture of people whom despised Americans. I'm happy to report these accusations could not be more wrong; everyone I encountered was exceptionally friendly and more than willing to dismiss my humble attempts at French. Once again, I have come to find, that as in every other aspect of life, you get what you give—and if you give people respect, regardless of their nationality, sex, or creed, you will usually get the same back.

Having eased my mind and broken down the walls of ethnic self-centeredness, I set out to see the sites of the much-heralded World's Most Romantic City. I did it all. At least as much as a married man who was alone in the World's Most Romantic City could do.

Being a good little tourist I went and visited the countryside and held the grapes of the vineyards between my fingers. I stood at the base of the Eiffel Tower and peered up her steel dress. I rode this great antique carousel that had tickets that felt like well-worn leather, and wooden horses that creaked as they did their routine dance number. I drank fine wines and ate an entire baguette for a snack. I toured the city and filled my eyes with the remarkable sights of the Louvre art museum and all her glorious treasures. I smiled back at the Mona Lisa. I stood triumphantly at the Arc de Triomphe. I walked through the shopping district, full of the hustle and bustle of life, overpriced hooker boots, and tight miniskirts. I said a prayer at the Notre Dame Cathedral and gazed up at the gargoyles as they kept their vigilant watch.

I somberly shuffled through the catacombs, which are filled with the earthly remains of people just like you and me. Remnants of those who once fell in love, had their hearts broken, and then fell in love again. The complex system of tunnels is filled with stacked bones and skulls of the deceased arranged in ornate patterns sometimes standing five feet high. The bones and skulls of people whom had jobs and bills, and more importantly, dreams; yet now, they are a mere tourist attraction, and from what I observed, were sadly being treated as such by tourists looking for a fun photo opportunity of them holding up a skull in a jovial fashion. In a few unfortunate cases, there were some people trying to smuggle out bones and skulls in their bags and jackets; quite the macabre souvenir and the ultimate sign of disrespect for the essence of human life if you ask me.

I was so overwhelmed with an inner sadness and emptiness that after mere minutes I had to make my way to the exit. To have gazed into the empty eye sockets of what was once someone's mother, wife or child, and then to see that very same piece of bone held up next to someone's face so that they could smile fool-heartedly and take a picture with it—it was just too much for me to emotionally digest.

I never touched a thing, not even grazed up against a stray piece of bone fragment. I did take a photo standing solemnly in one of the halls adjacent to the heroes of yesterday. Parents, friends, prom dates … loved ones. I wanted to capture the moment so that I might never forget how fragile life is, how each day truly is a great miracle. I hope to never forget that sadness, so that I may know the full joy of each day I am alive, and to always remember that each life should be respected. We are all important. No one more than another, but simply all of us, together, the human experience.

It is simply amazing to me that somehow there are still people in this world who do not see how we are all connected, and how we are all part of the same big picture. We are simple brush strokes upon the canvas of life, a dot on the Mona Lisa's brow. We are remarkably insignificant if we live only concerned with ourselves, no matter what your YouTube video, or your Twitter followers make you think.

Ah, Paris. The city above is so full of radiance, love, and beauty. Life the way life should be, for the living. And dwelling below the city is an area that should be sacred, respected, and left for the dead. To cross over and see people from above disrespecting the people down below was very disheartening. But what do I know. I spend a lot of time with the dead.

I do know this: The Paris catacombs should be, and could be, a monument and testament to human life, if only the living didn't screw it up.

Spain: A Lesson in Cartoons and Geography

My initial misconceptions of Spanish life I blame entirely on cartoons. As it turns out there aren't bullfights everywhere you go, and there is quite a remarkably noticeable absence of Mariachi bands and women dancing around hats underneath a waterfall of falling roses.

The fact that I originally thought Spain was in South America I blame partly on myself for not bothering to pay attention in geography. Although I believe some of the burden rests upon the shoulders of the self-centered culture that was widely in place, and thus taught to children, back in the 1980s.

At that time, America was winning on all fronts; you could sell blue jeans to the Russians for exorbitant prices, hair was best worn big, the Lambada was a forbidden dance, the hole in the o-zone layer was going to kill us all, Reagan was in the White House eating jelly beans, and the "Me Generation" was in full swing.

If it wasn't happening in America, then it just wasn't happening.

So, Spain could have been pretty much off the coast of my backyard and I wouldn't have bothered to notice. (Not that my backyard had a coast mind you. It did have a thin wooden fence to keep the ghetto out. The fence eventually broke and thus we had to move.)

Twenty years after the 1980s and the American dollar is hardly worth the paper it's printed upon, Russia could care less about our pants, the Lambada is a forgotten dance, global warming is going to kill us all, my hair is still big, Reagan is in the ground, and I am in Spain- which is near France and Portugal.

As it turned out, I had come a courting during the weekend of the Three Kings Holiday, which meant that pretty much everything was closed, in turn leaving little for me to do.

Strolling through Barcelona one could have thought there was a quiet apocalypse the night before, as only a few scattered souls were left shuffling through the wide city streets.

I decided to make the best of it and soak up as much of the culture and my surroundings that I could despite the absence of society and the presence of sobriety. It would be a little more difficult, but if one is careful and observant, much can be garnered by mere observation and a splash of inference.

The facade of the cityscape was quite striking. The layout of the buildings, the intersection of the streets, and the very essence of Barcelona itself, seemed to emanate a lust for life. A certain suaveness and quiet confidence is personified here, like the rhythmic swagger of a supermodel's hips as she struts down the runway of life. Spain is proud, self-assured, and straight up sexy.

Architecture reminiscent of the old world, rich with stone carvings and earthy tones, protected the heart of this passionate land. Dark reds and gleaming blacks were strikingly prominent in all facets of design, be it from the dress of the buildings to that of the people.

I know I was only imagining it, but the soft sounds of Spanish guitar in my mind made for a suitable soundtrack, and I would be willing to wager that had it not been a holiday weekend, I surely would have heard it echoing off the buildings somewhere in the distance.

But alas, the people of Barcelona, the lifeblood of Spain, were all at home with their families and I was left out in the rain- literally. The popular chorus of "My Fair Lady" is not true at all- the rain in Spain does not fall mainly on the plain- it rains everywhere- in bucket loads, and I was soaked in it.

There was one thing that was embraced by the people of Barcelona that I was aware of thanks to one of my most influential childhood teachers, Professor Bugs Bunny; perhaps you are familiar with his work.

Though there may not be Mariachi bands on the corner, dancing senoritas, and bull fights everywhere you look, there are in fact bulls; both snorting, charging kind, and of the decorative persuasion.

The proud and mighty image of the bull adorns t-shirts, foodstuffs, and various items available for purchase.

Driving along the motorways you will see various shadows of the darkest bulls punctuating the hillside. Enormous silhouettes of this signature animal are placed on farmland overlooking rolling fields of green and sandy browns.

Iconic in its strength, fiery passion, and suave appearance, the bull does well to encapsulate the people of Spain. Be it the actual land of Spain in Europe, the one I was misinformed about in South America, or the one that lives on in my animated mindscape.

A Fish Swims in Latvia

Let's get right to it for there is no sense in hiding it. I am a man who is having a love affair with breakfast. Be it pancakes, French toast, Belgian waffles, or simply an oversized plate of artery clogging bacon, there are few things I love more than a hot breakfast.

The odd thing is, when I am resting up at home, I hardly can ever be bothered to get out of bed and make a nice breakfast. I do, on rare occasion, rise early, and make a nice pancake breakfast for my wife and family. I like to add food coloring for the holidays. I try to make the pancakes into shapes, like hearts for Valentine's Day. I sometimes swirl a bunch of colors throughout the pancakes for a truly psychedelic breakfast experience. Those days aside, it's usually all I can do to scare up a bowl of delicious Boo Berry cereal to start my day.

On the road, however, I am a horse of another color but still of the same sex. I live for the free breakfast that can usually be found in the hotel lobby. Sometimes I cannot sleep in anticipation of it and will toss and turn while visions of fried eggs do the Lambada across the sticky kitchen floor tiles of my mind.

One plate of the hotel breakfast is never enough and so, to save time, I pile three to five plates high with fresh fruits, vegetables, eggs, bacon, and toast. In truth, it's not so much that I am a glutton, as it is that I simply don't like for a lot of my food liquids to get together. Syrup should not be on my fruit. Fruit juices should not be on my bacon. Speaking of bacon, sometimes I take bacon and three slices of bread and make a double-decker bacon sandwich. You have not lived until you have filled your mouth with as much bacon as it can possibly handle. Unless of course you are a vegetarian, then I am not sure how that translates. (I have so many vegan puns I could make, but I am afraid they would be in ... bad taste.)

I was just settling in for a nice breakfast in a Latvian hotel with my usual AM treats, when I caught a faint whiff of the sea coming from my plate. Being a native of Rhode Island, the Ocean State, I am usually quite fond of the salty brine scent, but not during breakfast.

I dismissed it as an early morning trick of the sinuses. However, with my first bite of pineapple, my tongue sent an email to my brain confirming that the sense of smell was not wrong. I believe the sense of smell may have been blind cc'd on the email as taste and smell seem to work together like that.

Usually, when I take a bite of pineapple, I am instantly whisked away to the tropical landscape of Hawaii. I can feel the soft warm sand betwixt my toes. I can see a fading orange sun melting into the ocean as my cares drift harmlessly out to sea. A tiny hula dancer with nice coconuts and a grass skirt moves her hips in a hypnotic rhythm that echoes deep within the caverns of my soul. Paradise.

However, this bite of pineapple simply induced the feeling of nausea. I couldn't understand how something so good could have gone so wrong. Who was it that tainted this sweet tart and seduced her out of her innocence?

Being a good little investigator, and none too bright, I decided to try another piece of the yellow fruit from my plate thinking the first one to be a fluke. It's like when you smell the milk, you know it's bad, and you still put it back in the fridge as if some dairy magician in a tall white hat is going to sneak in from behind the eggs and restore the milk to its once virgin-esque glory.

Once again, the pineapple disappointed me as the fishy taste rolled over my tongue like a capsized quahog boat. I felt like every pretty high school girl who repeatedly dated the guys that treated them like trash: Used, foolish, and utterly disappointed.

I moseyed back over to the fruit counter, mostly because it was still too early to saunter over to the fruit counter. Plus, moseying is much more manly. Moseying is to sauntering as John Wayne is to Richard Simmons.

As I observed the fruit counter I noticed that the pineapple was underneath a plastic cover, along with some snack cakes, and tiny little bowls of fish. I cannot tell you what type of fish it was as I refuse to eat anything from the sea, for in just my limited years on the planet, I have urinated in the ocean at least fifty-seven times, and counting. There are still decaying mobsters and remnants of dinosaur fecal matter floating around out there somewhere, and I will not eat from the world's toilet no matter how many times you flush it. Give me my pineapple bits and hula girl fantasy please.

The fishy after taste discouraged me from eating anything further, except for the bacon of course as the bacon was not under the little plastic dome and thus deemed safe by my senses. Once I was done with my patented double-decker bacon sandwich I decided to take a walk so that I might absorb the sights and sounds of Latvia and cleanse my palate.

The first thing that struck me about Latvia was its harsh winter winds. The cold pierced your skin like the sharp teeth of a great white shark. (Oh yeah—there's another reason I don't like to swim at the beach besides all the people peeing. Sharks!) Bundled up to the best of my ability, I continued on. The old impressions of Russia, which once had control of the Latvian people, were still visible. Deep red brick buildings were placed menacingly around the small town, as if still on guard, silently monitoring people through their vacant window eyes.

The people themselves were a mix of old-world culture and the Pepsi generation. Aged gentlemen with wind-scarred grimaces marched through the streets with great big fur hats atop their heads, earflaps pulled down tight. The young Latvian women strutted through the town in skin tight, 80's-esque acid washed jeans. Despite a language composed of letters that look abrasive themselves, the demeanor of the people was of a shy friendliness; like when a stray puppy who has come from a bad home approaches you for the first time. They appear careful and guarded, but once you scratch them behind their ears they warm right up to you. Of course, I was not going to scratch any Latvians behind their ears or under the earflaps of their hats for that matter, so a polite smile and friendly hello would have to suffice.

The icy waters of the Baltic Sea flow just outside of the town, and a wide river runs through it, that is, when the river is not frozen. When the river is frozen it's a whole different kettle of fish; which is a term that I never fully understood, but then again, I don't eat fish so it doesn't matter. Not fully grasping a turn of phrase is a small price to pay for not ingesting a creature that lives, swims, breathes, and eats in not only the waste of others, but also its own.

Upon the frozen river sat fisherman by the bucket load. Each one with his trusty pole in hand, hovering over his own small cut in the ice. It was unlike anything I had ever seen before and probably unlike anything I would ever see again. Sensing a rare opportunity, I decided to brave the cold and walk the riverbanks for a spell so that I may paint a more vibrant mental portrait to hang in my mind's gallery.

Some men fished in groups while others sought solace and isolated themselves in a remote location of the frozen river. No doubt each thought they had the best spot on the ice where fish would surely come.

As the ineffective sun began to set, lanterns popped on like stars in the sky, shining subtly across the shimmering surface of the frozen lake. There was a bridge that separated the upriver section from the lower where it spilled out eventually into the Baltic. You hate to see segregation amongst rivers, but they are making great strides towards unity, the wall between salt and fresh water coming down, sediment by sediment.

On the other side of the bridge the ice was not nearly as thick, and in some cases, was not frozen at all. In this area, the fishermen stood, lined up on both sides of the river. To my mind's eye it appeared as if they were all pall bearers and were shouldering their giant friend for one last walk.

I am a man who likes many things. Fish may not be one of them, but counting is. I think it goes back to my Sesame Street days that I spent in the castle with Count von Count. I challenged myself against the frigid temperatures to see if I could count how many people were braving the elements to pull in their catch, but between the darkness and the sheer mass of people it proved to be an impossible task. I would have to guess that there were easily 200 to 250 people out there casting their lines into the waters.

I climbed the frigid stone bridge and surveyed both sides for one last time. It was all so different from anything I had ever seen before. The communist type architecture, the extremely bitter cold, and all those ice fishermen out there, freezing their bottoms off for the very thing that ruined my sweet pineapple breakfast and Hawaiian girl fantasy. Well, at least they can't take bacon away from me.

Fairies, Ferries, and False Alarms

The Emerald Isle is full of enchanting tales, mysterious legends, and captivating myths. The only thing thicker than the folklore wrapped around the heart of Ireland is the luscious green grass that covers the land like a skim coat of expertly manicured pubic hair. If Mother Earth were a supermodel, Ireland would be her magical vagina that the other planets could only dream about.

Off the north coast of Ireland lays Rathlin Island, a small L-shaped piece of land, no longer than 2.5 miles and 4 miles wide. It comes complete with a pub, an inn, a few churches, sheep, cows, seals, and puffins. If you are unfamiliar with the majestic bird that is the puffin, simply picture the offspring of a penguin if it mated with a toucan. Or, if you like cartoon characters from the 80's and you know your cereal mascots, picture the offspring that would spring if Chilly Willy dipped his "willy" into someone's Froot Loops.

The island itself was once known as "Fairy Island" and is still regarded as such by some. "The Fey" is what you call the collective fairy folk of Ireland and this was a place they enjoyed.

To put your footprint on Rathlin Island you must first survive a ferry ride. Normally ferry rides are enjoyable and conjure up images of riverboat gambling, romance, and new beginnings. However, when you are attempting to power your way through the twisted currents of the Irish Sea as she battles with the fringes of the mighty Atlantic Ocean, it's not quite that easy.

The white capped waves and swirling whirlpools are enough to make sweat bead upon the brow of the most seaworthy of sailors; never mind landlubbers. Luckily, I have had the good fortune of growing up in a state known for its easy access to the sea and thus I have much boating experience, even working at a marine supply store for one lost summer of my youth. I wish I had that summer back. Perhaps I can consult a fairy.

Little did I know whilst staring out over the waters that this would be as close as I would have ever been to a tragic voyage. We weren't out of the harbor long before the swelling seas lapped at the sides of the boat like a thirsty cat's tongue in a water dish on a hot summer's day. The boat swayed from side to side, and rose and fell with each passing whim of King Neptune.

As water crashed over the sides of the vessel and across the main deck I began to ponder where the life jackets may be located and how long it would take me to find one. I am a decent swimmer and land was in sight on both sides, but with the turbulence of the ill-tempered waters that surrounded me, it appeared as if Mother Nature had PMS and I wasn't placing any bets on my backstroke to save my backside.

I had secured myself in the center of the boat figuring that if the worst were to come this would be my best chance at not getting caught in the undertow of the vessel as it capsized. Suddenly a thundering bolt of water struck us on the port side and water came pouring in. Aboard the boat was a small passenger vehicle whose tires squealed in fear as the car slid quickly across the deck. People scrambled as the boat groaned and creaked, tossed violently about like an ill-treated can of Yoo-Hoo in the hands of a hyperactive child.

Surely this was the scene of a movie playing out for the amusement of the gods. Now the only question was, what was my role? Was I to play the hero, the villain, a tragic character, or simply the plucky comic relief as per usual?

I prayed for the best and decided to make the most of it. If these were going to be my last moments on the planet I was going to enjoy it. I took my video camera out and went over to the side so that I may document the events as they would play out, and perhaps denote the final moments of my very existence. (How the camera may have survived a disaster at sea wile I did not, was a thought that never occurred to me- but hey- sometimes those things happen.)

Often, and most times so often that we tend to take them for granted, a miracle occurs. The seas suddenly calmed, all was well and we had arrived at Rathlin Island.

As the scratchy sand scrubbed up against the sides of the boat's hull, yet another small part of the Almighty's plan had unfolded. After being shepherded safely across violent waters I thought briefly of the words to Amazing Grace. Yet again, a wretch like me hath been saved.

But for how long would our hero or plucky comic relief character remain safe? (I must be one or the other. I really can't see myself as a villain. A tragic character maybe- I don't know how the story ends yet- but never a villain.)

My time on the island was quite pleasant and a tad mysterious, but such is the way of Ireland. A few days into the trip, whilst recalling my nautical adventure and taking an incredibly hot shower, as I am known to do, the fire alarm in the hotel went off. I figured the fairies were playing fairy games, as the folks of Ireland believe them to do.

Knowing that my room had a small balcony of sorts, and that I was on the first floor above ground level, I did not panic. I have had enough training in fire services to get myself out of this one if need be. So, I promptly finished my exfoliation and slipped out of the shower curtain to wrap myself in a warm towel as the alarm siren blared its tireless warning again and again to the disdain of my eardrums.

I was barely able to dry my nether region when my hotel door burst open and in walks the gentleman from the front desk. The steam from my shower was so incredibly intense that it had in fact triggered the smoke alarm.

You can imagine my embarrassment- but at least I had that warm towel to shield me from his curious eyes. Seriously, this guy was hanging around a little too long for a false alarm.

Alas, after a few days of several trying encounters and having neither met my maker by water or fire, I decided to mosey over to the pub and hoist a pint to The Fey, to the fairies of fairy island- and to being the plucky comic relief character once again. Maybe someday I'll be the hero, but never the villain. That is something to be proud of.

Prague: Jazzy by Day – Classy by Night

Somewhere in Prague, located in the heart of the "Old Town" sits the often-visited Charles Bridge. It was constructed in the 15th century and is historically important, as it was not just the only way to cross the River Vltava, but it was considered immeasurably valuable in its use for trade in the 1500s. Three towers guarded the Charles Bridge; two on the side of the Prague Castle, and one on the other, near the Old Town. She, and the people who walk upon her, are also watched over by the 30 statues of Saints that adorn her mighty stone crest.

On the Charles Bridge by day you will see marionette puppets being manipulated to dance and to entertain. Sketch artists are dutifully shading the faces of young girls in fun caricatures and hiding the wrinkles of older ladies in charcoal portraits. Those leather bracelets and crystal amulets that you will wear for a week or two and then throw into your bottom drawer, they are available for purchase here. Children run noisily past with their dripping ice cream cones. The elderly slowly rub the plaque below the statue of Saint John of Nepomuk, in hopes that their prayers to cure their aching joints will soon be answered.

A constantly flowing sea of humanity, each person vying for a better photo opportunity, push and squeeze their way along the bridge. Seeing life through a viewfinder, through a lens, through the stories of paid tour guides whom carry umbrellas so you can see them over the massive crowd.

In the background stands a charming old man with a straw hat. He performs as an organ grinder, his melody filling the air and creating an old-timey type atmosphere that somehow appropriately fits with the gothic landscape of castle tops, church spires, and guard towers. Atop his decorative music box sits a little stuffed monkey instead of a real one, but no one seems to mind.

Further down the bridge I stumbled upon a very entertaining little band, which simply brought a smile to my face. So much so, that I took up residence there, perched on the bridge wall behind them, just to listen for a while and let them record the soundtrack for this memory in the making.

They played jazz music, but not the trendy want to be hip type of jazz that guys play in their bedrooms to try and impress young ladies and coerce them into dropping their underpants. No, this wasn't that type of dirty seductive jazz accompanied by lava lamps, silk sheets, and that faint latex smell of condoms. This wasn't like that at all.

This was in the style of the early 40's. This was more like the type of jazz that they played in old Merrie Melodies Cartoons- my favorite kind of cartoons.

It was near impossible not to close my eyes and see that little boy I used to be, peering up under his over-grown bowl cut, eyes fixated on the television screen, his hand wrapped around the large soup spoon, moving methodically back and forth from mouth to cereal bowl and back again. Back in the good ole days, back when the world was big and I was little.

Yet, I could not close my eyes to the seven men whom sat in front of me with clarinets, French horns, an upright bass, and various other instruments; massaging each note gently out into the world, giving birth to a swinging little Jazz baby.

Young girls with flowing hair would walk up and stop there as if hypnotized; wry, playful little smiles upon their face. Flirting with the old men for just a moment, swooning to these heroes of yesterday before they went back on their way.

What a moment to behold.

I stared up at the pitchforked peaks of the surrounding buildings. I looked down into the strong currents of the river. I missed the little boy sitting too close to the TV, his mouth full of more sugar than Rice Krispies. I watched as the old men passed the hat. I bought a CD of the Original Prague Syncopated Orchestra and headed back to my hotel.

I wondered what magic the bridge held at night and I made a mental sticky note to return after the sun had said its prayers. Also on the sticky note was a reminder to buy more Nutella, as I had been recently developing a love for its sensational blend of hazelnuts, milk, and cocoa. When mixed with peanut butter it is damn near orgasmic, or at the very least, it's like that funny feeling I get when I smell fresh paint on a breezy spring day or see those large Christmas lights from the 1980s.

Alas, sandwich spreads and sexual turn-ons aside, I returned to the Charles Bridge that very evening.

Beneath a starry sky the bridge takes on a completely different tone; like a housewife getting dressed up for a night on the town, pausing just slightly as she catches herself in the mirror when she clasps a string of pearls around her neck; the long black evening gown reminiscent of the woman she remembers fondly.

The moon shines down upon the Charles Bridge, just illuminating the tips of the stone angels' wings as they stand watch over the travelers. Her small square cobblestones that have once again bore the weight of many a tourist, breathe tiny sighs of relief for another day over and a job well done.

And then, when it seems all is finished for the day, he quietly appears. A small man with large round glasses and disheveled hair quietly takes to the scene. His tweed coat seems to hang down just a bit below where it should, as if, despite his age, he is still wearing his older brother's hand-me-downs. His watery eyes, magnified by the seemingly oversized glasses, look focused, but on a very faraway place; not here. He appears almost as a mouse that was turned into a man for just this one night, for just this one occasion, here in this enchanted land of Prague.

He carries with him a small black case and an even tinier black bag. Out of the bag he extracts and sets up two candles at either end of the small black case. Stepping back slowly, he opens the case. With the care of a mother cradling her newborn baby, he gently carries out a chestnut colored violin. He dips his chin down low, holding her in place, firmly, but not too tight, like a gentle lover. He strikes up his bow quickly and then hesitates. The moment is almost perfect. Slowly drawing it across the strings, the saddest, yet most beautiful song fills the night sky like a pillowy-soft bosom in a low-cut evening gown.

How can something so faint, played by a man so demure, suddenly appear so large as to encompass the entire bridge and all whom stroll upon its rocky path? Young lovers stop and kiss, old couples hold hands and think of all the years they have been together. The good times, the disappointing times, the trying times, these last times. Lonely-hearts shuffle by softly focused upon the longing of their own minds.

As the flames of the mouse-man's candles flickered and danced across the shadows of the night sky, I couldn't help but wonder how many before me have witnessed this breath-taking sight. How many have strolled this very path, arm in arm with the one they loved? Have made wishes on the plaques of the saints or perhaps upon the stars above?

There was an undefined enchantment to the moment. A moment I knew I would never have opportunity to be witness to again. The way the winds themselves appeared to stand still. The way the river waters below seemed to calm. The gray eyes of the statues almost saddened for their current immobile state.

The crowded bridge of the day, the town itself, all seemed empty somehow, and the world, well the world seemed big again. Full of hope, of promise, and a hint of mystery; of things still yet to be discovered. A prize nestled in the bottom of the sugary cereal box for the boy with the over-sized bowl cut.

Majestic Mauterndorf

As if lying in a hammock betwixt the Austrian hillside, the sleepy little town of Mauterndorf appears content to just be, and to let the warm breezes glide over and caress her like the gentle hand of an experienced and trusted lover. No safe word is needed here.

Beneath a sky of the softest baby blues, I found myself wandering a forest path set beside a rolling stream. The water could not have been clearer, magnifying the smooth stones that lie beneath its relaxing flow; washing away all sin and impurity, all marks of troubled times and hardship, an unbiased baptism for all.

A bed of a million pine needles made for the softest cushion to walk upon as I strolled deeper into the verdant patchwork of trees and fields that made up the ground floor of the picturesque landscape's hillside high-rise.

Sheep bleated, horses neighed, and curious rabbits took one final look at this stranger among them before turning their tails to the wind and disappearing into the forgiveness of the tree cover. There is so much life to behold and yet only one lifetime to do it in, one must have a patient and careful eye to truly capture it all.

The Austrian hillside is a virtuous young lady dancing with the moon and picnicking with the sun. And to a boy raised within the cold and decaying concrete jungles of American suburbia, it was hard to even imagine places like this were still in existence.

Here, the world feels like it did when you were a child; big and full of wonder, hope, promise, and mystery. I walked on and let the sun heal my homesick heart, the sounds of the stream comfort my soul, and the winds carry my troubles to the heavens.

If the air outside were capable of smelling like fresh, clean cotton sheets, this would be the scent of Mauterndorf, with all its comforts and joys. The air so pure and sweet, with just a touch of blooming tulips, conjured up words like untainted and virgin-esque, but even they seem to pale in comparison to this wondrous beauty; as if one were to say that the magnificent Miss Marilyn Monroe was simply "cute."

Small dark houses with rustic features reminiscent of the old world are far spread throughout the land; each one adorned in a soft shroud of purple and yellow flowers, adding to the quilt of color that comforts this land.

Even the dandelion, a weed of discontent back home, appear majestic among its flower brethren as they heartily are interwoven with the lush green blades of grass upon the slopes of the hills.

Lost in the hillside and in thought, I could almost see myself in my youth, staring out from under that bowl cut hairstyle, if you could even call it that, standing shyly with a whole new chance at peace, at life, at myself, before becoming a man these many years later.

If ever there were a place that truly seemed removed from modern society, free of its scrutiny, hardships, and prejudices, it is the simple town of Mauterndorf.

Majestic Mauterndorf—where the world is still big, where there still exists plenty of room for the dreams and hopes of that child in all of us; where the dandelion is free to be a flower.

Bloody History, Pointed Hats and Unique Views

They say that Rome wasn't built in a day, but when you are traveling through the Italian countryside on a hurried schedule, well, sometimes you have to try and see it all in a day. I would have to board a train in the famed city of Pisa to begin my journey, however I would be remiss to skip over a viewing of the famed leaning tower and so the crooked icon of Italy was my first stop.

Funny enough, the old gal was under construction at the time, scaffolding obscuring a section of her torso. But nonetheless, there she stood, resiliently against the laws of gravity and nature, a black eye that at one time no one wanted to talk about, now an unsung hero in the war against normality. The gray lady stands in the plaza as a seemingly contradictive statement, like a crucifix adorning the neck of a lady of the night, but then again, Jesus loves us all, as well we should.

Visitors and locals alike gathered around her mighty trunk and stared up at the heavens beyond her tilted top, while I lay there in the shade staring up her dress. The fine sculpture that she is, the elegant tower stands in solitude with a certain air of whimsy and an aftertaste of classic romance. I find the Tower of Pisa to be an inspiration, a lesson to behold. For even when things don't seem to work out as we had hoped and planned, we must play the hand we are dealt and always keep in mind that we are not privy to viewing the larger picture that is life. And that sometimes, challenging conventional thought, going against the grain and being true to one self is not only a good thing but also what is necessary. Don't be afraid to be different. Don't obsess with perfection.

On the train ride to Rome my head was filled with the snippets of documentary and movie footage that make up my mental history of the mighty Coliseum and the noble Vatican.

As a fourth-generation Italian-American, which basically means I am a straight up American Mixed Breed, I have always desired to see the curved façade of the Coliseum. I wanted to behold in my eyes the place where talented gladiators fought and where brave Christians gave their lives. And as with everything else, in every society in every time, the great division of the classes; the nobility of Rome seated up high, while the ever-struggling middle class strived to just stay out of the ghetto.

Walking down the old stone streets just outside of the Coliseum walls, you can almost hear the horses pulling the wooden chariots as they clap and slide across the rocks. The forceful tones of the Roman soldiers as they shouted at the crowds still play across the drive-in movie screen of one's mind.

Alas, times have changed, and the new citizens of Rome are beeping the horns on their scooters and the only yelling being done is by street vendors selling plastic gladiator swords for the kids to battle each other, and brightly colored paper umbrellas for the ladies to fight with the sun.

But beyond all the scooters, the vendors, the traffic, and the crowds, quietly stands the shadow of a giant, a peaceful warrior, now in its golden years.

The once blood thirsty Coliseum now appears gentle, thoughtful, and full of the echoes of yesteryear; like an old war hero sitting in the corner of the nursing home, praying desperately that people will still come and visit. A humble colossus being pumped full of life by an I.V. of tourism dollars; clinging to life and trying against all hope not to fade into obscurity and slip quietly into nothingness; a crooked, toothless smile upon its face.

A leisurely walk through the streets of Rome brought me past colorful gift shops, quaint outdoor cafes, and numerous fountains lined with smooth marble statues; tourists dipping their feet in the crystal waters.

Arriving at Vatican City on a whim almost seems unfair in comparison to the pilgrimage of a lifetime that it is for so many others. But, we all have our own paths, our own destinies and our own strokes of luck, and being able to walk through the hallowed halls of the Vatican Church is part of my story.

There was a small line that led to a metal detector and security checkpoint, and so I waited patiently. It would seem inappropriate to become agitated in such a place, especially when you are waiting in line with little white-haired grandmas and nuns whose hair was tucked neatly under habits.

I was a tad bit conflicted upon going further into the Vatican. Personally, I have always quietly rallied against the position of the Pope. I have nothing against any Pope; I just don't like the hierarchy of it all. God is the King, that's good enough for me. Maybe I just don't like authority figures or middle management.

Truthfully, I am just not in agreement with manmade decrees on behalf of God.

I don't believe that any man has a greater ability to speak for God just because he wears a pointy hat. But that's just me and I don't wear hats very much.

After clearing my conscience and security I paused for just a moment before entering the holy cathedral.

In a way, it was like losing your spiritual virginity; you can only do it once for the first time, so why rush?

I gazed up at the expertly carved, dark wooden doors that guarded the threshold. My mind pondered all that it meant to be at the doorway to the Vatican Church regardless of my viewpoints on the papacy and papal doctrine. Still wrestling with my own thoughts, I bowed my head like a child going to the Principal's office and shuffled undeservedly through the entrance.

I felt the slippery marble floor glide effortlessly beneath the soles of my sneakers. I felt the stillness of the air as the hair on my arms stood at attention like a thousand tiny soldiers. I felt lightheaded.

Before my eyes was one of the most immaculate sights that I have ever had the pleasure to behold. Like Linus in the pumpkin patch, there was truly not a sign of hypocrisy as far as the eye could see, nothing but sincerity and wonder.

Suddenly, I felt incredibly out of place and underdressed, like a young man showing up for a first date with the high school hottie, only to realize you have left the tags on your jeans and there are sweat stains on your shirt. Or like showing up for a job interview in a blazer and jeans and then being interviewed by a high-powered player in a three-piece suit and golden cuff links that are worth more than your truck.

First dates are a lot like job interviews I think. Pretty much you are trying to convince someone that you are worthy of his or her time and the awards the come with the desired position, even though you know deep inside that you are extremely under qualified and that your resume is a pack of lies.

There I stood amidst the Super Bowl of Catholicism, wearing a Pink Floyd T-Shirt, ripped jeans, and a pair dirty high tops. Well, I was made in God's image, right?

Alas, I tried to take comfort in the fact that though I may look a little rough around the edges, my soul was clean, and I think that is what the Big Guy would care the most about.

Once inside I found an unspeakable calmness descend upon me, and just like that I was at peace with myself and was astonished at the simple beauty of it all.

I have been in many churches throughout the world of much less notoriety that were decorated to the hilt with gold leaf and crystal. Yet, here in the Vatican, there was a very notable absence of all that pomp and circumstance and it seemed appealing to my inner nature.

White marble cherubs danced with dark wooden carvings of Christ, all beneath a painted ceiling that seemed as if it touched the heavens themselves. Sunbeams of pure white light shone brightly upon the altar and spotlighted a statue of Mary.

I knelt at the prayer stations, I stared at the paintings, I ran my hands across the sculptures, and I quietly watched the people of God pray. It was easy to feel small here, the way you should feel in the presence of God; humbled, inspired and thankful.

I left the Vatican feeling thoughtful. For all its beauty and its significance, it is a place that has a very troubled past, but then again, don't we all, and isn't that in part what it means to be human.

It's how we learn from our past, deal with our mistakes, and approach our future that matters, for truly none of us are perfect.

Throughout my travels in Italy, I had seen some very important structures that spoke to key points in history and in life.

Within the walls of the Coliseum many battles have been fought for the amusement of men who made themselves gods.

At the Vatican, men have caused even more bloodshed and have done so in the name of God.

In truth, despite their varying approach, I dare say their pasts are not quite as different as they would like the world to believe. However, the Vatican and Catholicism have persevered in part due to their ability to learn from their mistakes and to move forward.

Across the hills of Italy, nestled within valleys and hidden behind shadows, the Coliseum stands as a symbol of the brutal history of humanity; the Vatican as a beacon of Faith and hope for a better tomorrow; and the leaning tower of Pisa as a reminder to just be who you are, that there is beauty in imperfection- and to do the best you can, for sometimes that is truly all we can do.

A Crosswalk Opportunity

At first glance the country of Chile appears to be nothing more than an alternative version of Miami. There are tall buildings that were once white in color, miles of beachfront that were once covered with pristine granules of sand, and lots and lots of people which appear to be simply marring up the rest of what was once a beautiful landscape.

Horns are blaring; buses are packed to the gills, motorcycles dart to and fro between the traffic, and a sea of humanity ebbs and flows over the cracked sidewalks. It appears as if the land itself has simply acquiesced to the overpowering human condition. What can possibly control this seemingly overwhelming nightmarish chaos?

Then it happens; the traffic lights turn yellow, and then red. Vehicles screech to a halt. The smell of rubber, oil, and brake pads mixes to form a veritable automobile potpourri. With the blink of a light, the humanoids waiting for the walk signal suddenly sprint out into the street to gain a step or two on their competition.

With a bit of a swagger, a once young girl caked in clown makeup steps into the crosswalk and turns to face the halted traffic. She lights aflame the baton from behind her back and tosses it, ten, fifty, twenty feet into the air! Catching it each time without the hint of fear. She bats it back and forth, under her legs, over her shoulders and around her back. She sees the walk signal start to blink faster out of the corner of her eye and so she quickly puts out the flames- with her tongue. She takes off her comically oversized top hat and walks to the cars as they roll down their windows and pitch a peso or two into the black magic hat.

She is just one of the many Chilean street performers- a proud and eccentric guild.

They wait at the busiest of intersections wanting only to entertain and to collect a small toll before the traffic whooshes by once again, returning the drivers back to the market, the office, the bar, and back to their mundane life.

At the stoplight, there is a bit of whimsy, of disbelief, of grandeur, as many different performers of all ages, shapes, and sizes wait quietly for their moment to entertain.

Some juggle rubber balls; some do gymnastics, others an urban ninja type display jumping off steps, traffic dividers and sometimes the cars themselves. They range from the mundane to the flamboyant, but each one stands their posts and performs their routines with the same enthusiasm for countless hours on end.

Some dress extravagantly in makeup and sequins, while others simply wear street clothes. One young gentleman was decked out in a tuxedo. Regardless of attire, it's the same discipline to the traffic light to which they all show dutiful respect.

The audience sit in their cars and, for the most part, seem to enjoy the rituals; gladly handing a few coins out of the window in trade for a few minutes' entertainment, a mild distraction from their droll commute. The only beeping you may hear is from the bus drivers when the performers take up a little too much of the fresh green while trying to collect some coins.

If you observe this ritual and the reaction to it, you will quickly see that the people of Chile themselves are the very lifeblood and essence of the land. Sure, the pollution of the massive number of vehicles is a problem. Of course, with so many people come trash, litter, sweat and blood stains. But without them, there would be no one to visit the tall buildings, no one to sit on the sandy beaches, no one to perform in the streets, and no one to entertain. It would all be one big lost opportunity, and the young clown girl would have no reason to use her soft pink tongue to extinguish the hot orange flames, and no reason to dance in the crosswalk as the streets of Chile would be empty and saddened.

Sometimes things are meant to be taken out of the package. Sometimes things are meant to fall apart. Sometimes, you have to do what you do and take advantage of a captive audience.

The Sideshow by the Seashore

Along the coast of Argentina's saltwater Lake Mar Chiquita, meaning "Little Sea", the town of Miramar sits vacant as the autumnal breezes dance and play through the empty streets like a carefree child in the park.

Miramar is a summer resort, a vacation destination, and a simple beach town if you will. And like most places of similar description, when the cold weather moves in, the visitors move out. What remains is a desolate place, reminiscent of an amusement park in the wee hours of the morning; a giant Ferris wheel looming in the dawn like a lonely, shadowy giant.

Beachfront cottages are abandoned. Their walkways thickly covered with the last overgrowth of the season. Powder blue painted plywood covers the windows of trinket shops and ice cream parlors. Wide mouth streets are left thirsty, longing for the days under the hot sun. Dogs lazily lie about in the roads without concern for the one or two cars that will cross their path throughout the entire day. The term ghost town isn't entirely appropriate, but it does come to mind.

If you squint your mind's eye you can almost see the throngs of people packing the store sidewalks or laying sprawled out on the sands like a faded scrapbook memory in sepia tone. Transparent images lost in time, forgotten faces of yesterday, lost summer romances of yesteryear.

There are still a few small shops open for the locals who live here year-round; most of them proprietors of another store themselves. A restaurant or two opens for a few hours here and there, with a limited menu and limited service.

The local bar is more rightly described as having a few beers and playing pool in the spare room of a buddy's house. The setting is informal; children sit and watch the Disney channel and do their homework while you sip a lukewarm beer in the chilly night air.

The police routinely patrol the area, but it seems to be out of mere boredom more than anything else. They wave friendly hellos to the fishermen who sit upon the rock wall, casting their lines into the water, and reeling in the night.

For now, things are simpler here, people friendlier, and life is taken at a slower pace.

All that will change come the next summer, when the bright sun smiles overhead, and young love blossoms like a teenage girl's bosom in the training bra world below.

But for now, in the crisp air, it's okay to take your time, to let your mind wander and to dream of a far-off place.

It is Miramar in the off-season; a vacant playground, a quiet carousel, an empty shoebox of yellowing love letters and fading memories.

One of my fading memories. This little pup followed me around the town of Miramar, and even crashed with me at my beach cottage. I called her Sassy.

Australia: Land of Contrast

Back in 1980s America there existed a tangible fascination with Australia and all things down under. From Paul Hogan and his adventures in the Crocodile Dundee series to Men at Work singing about vegemite sandwiches, things were going well for the reputation of those from the former penal colony.

Twenty years later, long after the initial wave of Aussie interest, I finally made my way to the Outback. Well, maybe I stayed in Sydney and therefore not technically brush country, but it was close enough to travel to the neighboring towns and check off items on my faded yellow, mental sticky note of things that needed to be seen should I ever make my way to Australia.

The note read as follows:

Boomerangs

Aboriginal Culture

Didgeridoos (The low-pitched wind instrument)

Vegemite

The Sydney Opera House

The Harbor Bridge

Koalas

Bandicoots

Wombats

A Dingo (Preferably not eating a baby)

Kangaroos

A cliché list indeed, but I figure that the rest of what Australia had to offer would work itself out naturally and bond the whole experience together like Play-Doh in shag carpeting.

I was barely off the plane and saw the first item on my list, boomerangs. Every traveling parent and grandparent must buy these things and bring them back to their kids and grandkids alike, and thus you really can't throw one without hitting a store that sells them and returning with a receipt for $5.95.

After settling at the hotel and making my way to the Sydney harbor I was all set to hit the streets with my camera, ready to document the Aussie experience.

Just a few steps out into the harbor and something in the air seemed familiar, yet I could not quite place it. Step after step through the busy Sydney streets brought me closer and closer to this illusive, yet familiar, phantom.

I looked into shops and bought some postcards and t-shirts. I stopped at an outdoor market and bought a delicious Black Angus steak sandwich from a tall Australian gentleman with dirty blonde hair that was matted with sweat and stuck to his forehead. I also purchased a chocolate fudge brownie from a small, older Asian woman who lured me in with a free sample on a toothpick. I have always been a sucker for a free sample and food on a stick. Someone must have told her I was coming. Suddenly I found my belly filled with warmth and a sense of hope, which is an odd sensation for food to bring; yet it somehow was there.

Fueled up and ready to continue, I slowly made my way down to where the Opera House is viewable. Tourists were lined up along the waterfront snapping a photograph in front of one of the most recognizable structures the world has to offer. One simple picture-something to frame and put in your cubicle to remind yourself that indeed there is more outside of those fabric-covered walls, those 9-5 prisons.

I was impressed at the sheer size of the harbor itself. To my left stood the Harbor Bridge, stretched mightily across the blue and green waters of the Pacific Ocean. The waves gently lapping up alongside the white clamshell-esque structure of the Opera House on my right.

Funny how the mind works sometimes, or in my case, most the times; I was suddenly transported back to my childhood, watching the ball drop in Times Square on television on New Year's Eve. They would show clips from celebrations across the world and every year they would show Sydney Harbor, with fireworks exploding into furious reds and brilliant whites over the bridge and the opera house. Years later I would find myself working in the news business for CBS and FOX television, editing that very same video footage as a show editor, and then eventually back to watching it yet again, this time from the back of a Live truck as a field photographer. And yet, that, all of that, all of it was a distant memory as I stood betwixt the monumental bosom of Lady Sydney herself, no longer watching it on a television monitor but for the first time, staring at it through my own eyes, not through someone else's lens.

Suddenly an escaping sense of home had struck. I thought it was perhaps the salt air of the ocean wafting on the breeze that was causing the phenomena, but I have traveled many places before that border various bodies of salt water and none of them have brought me as close to home as this. It must be something else. I dismissed it.

A steady techno beat mixed with the unmistakable throaty tones of the didgeridoo lured me away from the waterfront and over to a gentleman, painted up like a traditional Aborigine, whom was seated playing the instrument to a small crowd. He had his obligatory hat for collecting donations as well as a stack of CDs for sale.

Funny thing about this man and his "didgeridoing"—it never stopped, even when his lips went from the mouthpiece to a cigarette. It would prove to be that this man was no more a native than I was, and that his music was lip-synched, if in fact one can lip sync a didgeridoo musical movement.

A little disheartened, but nonetheless able to check off another item on my list, I continued out of the town and further into the countryside. There I was witness to numerous wombats, though unfortunately they were all deceased and laying in various contorted positions along the roadside. Curious looking little creatures though, as if a small bear had mated with a gopher, and was then hit with a vehicle traveling at high speeds. It is said that one in five accidents in Australia is wildlife related, and I could see why. I wondered what insurance premiums were like.

Alive or dead, another item had been checked off the mental sticky note of things to see should I ever make my way to Australia. Koala's however, were proving to be difficult to locate despite my staring into the roadside treetops for countless moments. Dingos were another creature that were eluding both my contact and camera lenses. Speaking of camera lenses, the bandicoot is an interesting little animal indeed, as it is actually against the law to photograph it if you are using a flash. Apparently, the bright flash scares the little critters to death, literally. I suppose you can't through them surprise parties either. As a child, I had a beagle named Belvedere that we would throw surprise birthday parties for. He would get a meatball with a candle in it instead of a cake. I had to blow out the candle. He got to eat the meatball.

Back in Australia I was counting the white dividing lines as they clicked past the grill of the car, noting another mile traveled, another minute of my life rushed past. I began to whimsically gaze up into the passing hillsides. Some were so steep that they seemed to pierce the sky itself. Things were different here, the clouds seemed whiter and purer; the sky more blue and tranquil. The stark contrast between the brown and yellow hills and the passing heavens was unreal- it was like watching a 3-D movie but without the special glasses and over-priced popcorn that vary by size and twenty-five cents. Words, no matter how flowery, simply cannot do the beauty of Australia justice. It was as if my eyes had lost their virginity and were passionately in love.

The white lines slowed as I stopped at a roadside store where I saw jars of Vegemite. Let's just say it must be an acquired taste that I have yet to acquire. I may live out the rest of this life without ever acquiring such a taste, but at least I could cross it off my list.

Back on the road it became increasingly apparent that Dingos were also going to be something I would not be able to acquire upon this trip. Kangaroos however, made up for it. They were in abundance, both hopping along the roadside, and in some cases, laying lifeless on the blacktop, like furry refrigerators thrown out of a truck. I seriously underestimated the size of kangaroos.

In the coming days, I was even able to playfully chase some kangaroos across a golf course on a cart that I borrowed from some kind golfers. I personally don't play golf, unless there are windmills and clowns involved, so my day on the green was spent mingling amongst kangaroos and snapping pictures.

With my Aussie experience ending I found myself in want for more. Such a distant place that somehow reminded me of home I had never seen. The impressive landscapes, the various wildlife, the vibrant city life, the cold death, the elusive feeling of familiarity, it was all here in the down under, on the other side of the world, far from anything I had known or could have ever imagined.

Animation, Self-Gratification, and Appreciation

It is a pretty sad realization in the life of a man, or a woman for that matter as I do not think the presence of breasts and a vagina change the scenario at all, anyhow, regardless of what may or may not lie betwixt your legs, it is a pretty sad realization in one's life when they must admit to themselves and whomever else bothered to ask, that the only thing they know about Tasmania, is based upon the whirling, frothing, eating machine as depicted in the Warner Bros. cartoons of yesteryear.

Yet there I was, humbled at the age of 32 years, having to admit that once again, my knowledge is most heavily derived from glimpses of reality, immensely saturated by animation, and influenced by commercial jingles.

With such helpful insight as "the Tasmanian Devil eats pretty much everything (especially wabbits)," I struck out on my sojourn through the rural backwoods of Tasmania. A mere flight from the coast of Australia, through some of the highest regularly noted winds at airports worldwide, and there I was in cartoon land with not a cross-dressing rabbit in sight.

The weather was crisp and cool, it reminded me of Thanksgiving morning back in New England, without the sweet smell of turkey, without the comfort of warm mashed potatoes, without the parade, and without the people for that matter. In a word, the place appeared nearly desolate, a losers' Thanksgiving at best.

I ended up spending a lonely soul searching week in a very isolated spot just outside of historic Port Arthur, known for being a vast prison complex which Australia, a formal penal colony itself, sent its own prisoners; Outcasts amongst outcasts; Misfits amongst misfits. Tasmania: the original Isle of Misfit Toys. Where was King Moon Racer when you needed him?

I toured the prison grounds of Port Arthur. I visited the buildings and read the informative placards as I strolled throughout the sprawling settlement. Not wanting to spend any more time than I needed to in prison, I used my handy get out of jail free card which I won when I landed on Free Parking, and I made my way to see the much-heralded Tasmanian Devil at a nature preserve. The furry little creatures looked nothing like their animated cousin out in Hollywood.

If it was physically possible for a bear to mate with a hamster, assuming they were both in love and of legal consenting age, the Tasmanian Devil might be what such a romantic union would produce.

The Devil looked about the size of a large housecat or a small dog, depending on if you are a cat person or a dog person; I make the analogies, you decide what works best for you.

Black and white, with wiry looking fur and strong snapping jaws, the Tasmanian Devil makes a living eating whatever is thrown at it. And usually, food is thrown at it thanks to their biting nature. Unfortunately, they are a dying breed due to a specific cancer, which they have been passing around to each other through their constant biting and bickering. To preserve the species, some of the healthy ones now live in captivity and are fed scraps of meat and bone. And yes, they do eat bone and all. The snapping and popping sounds are immense as they tear through their meals. If only the Mafia knew of such an animal, they could have saved a fortune on cement shoes.

A series of photos, a stroll through the kangaroo farm where you can pet these tame creatures that were rescued from roadside accidents, and I was on my way back to my room, burdened with the knowledge that I had spent more time talking to the animals than I did with people. Look out Dr. Doolittle! You have competition!

The little hotel was nestled in a woody area that very much resembled the hairy patches of a fat man's belly, sporadically placed and seemingly without any good reason. The place was decent enough though, as most rooms for rent are. I had a couch, a hot water kettle, a mini fridge, a shower, and a queen size bed. Pretty much the necessities were supplied; all except for heat, oddly enough. I was given an electric blanket however, which warmed my weary bones and comforted my soul at the end of the day, bringing me back to my childhood nights, snuggled up in my feety-pajamas and toasty warm blankey.

Many moons had passed since I was as a kid, wide-eyed and innocent. Sneaking out of bed in the late hours of the night when everyone was asleep in hopes of catching a glimpse of any R-rated movie that might be so kind as to even cast a brief flicker of boob across my pre-pubescent gaze. Ah childhood, how fleeting; animation by day and gratification by night. My mind like a sponge, absorbing whatever clues of culture and cubes of knowledge television was offering whilst scrubbing away my innocence like an unwanted bit of broccoli from the dinner plate. (Which I still choose not to eat.)

Alas, there was nothing to watch on the two channels Tasmanian TV had to offer, so I stepped out for a walk in the night air, looking up to the moon shining sadly in the sky like a lonely prostitute on Valentine's night. Every business has an off-season, even the world's oldest profession.

Whilst walking, I stumbled across a sign for a place called Pirate's Bay, and being a modern-day plunderer and pillager, I decided it was only natural that I should wander that way. It was peaceful, it was empty, and it was like sitting too close to a movie screen. My vision was filled from corner to corner with stars and the reflection of stars as they danced and played upon the waves. The Southern Cross constellation shown mightily in the dark sky, an "X" marking the spot I was meant to be in at that moment in time, at that page in the dime-store pulp fiction novel of my life.

I felt small, as one should feel. There was a glimmer of innocence reflected upon the crests of the waves. A hint of hope hung silently in the night air as to not give away the future, but just enough to make sure you continue to play the game. Maybe it was because I hadn't really seen many people in a few days' time that I was so thoughtful. Maybe it was because I had found a scorpion in my sneaker earlier in the morning, just as I was about to slip my foot inside. Maybe it was because we are not meant to know all that is going on, and much like sitting too close to the movie screen it prevents us from seeing the whole picture, leaving us with nothing to do but wonder and ask questions and sneak out of our rooms late at night to glimpse a brief smattering of skin on, the appropriately named, "boob tube".

Whatever the reason was, I suddenly found myself thinking more about the big picture of life, and how each day is truly a blank canvas to be thankful for, whether the picture turns out to be a masterpiece or a complete disaster. It's our masterpiece, our disaster, and as long as there is breath in our lungs, we have the chance to create once again tomorrow.

We can continue to try, to hope and to play the game, or we can continue to grunt and groan, piss and moan, and slowly bite each other into extinction.

As for me, I'm going to paint my future.

Life Flashes Before Your Eyes, Indeed

It was a crazy day amongst a series of crazy days somewhere in 2009. I was an unwilling passenger in a runaway vehicle that would merely be the first of many a harrowing ride that I would take during my visit to Malaysia.

Though the variables always changed, car models, drivers, different routes, and destinations, there was one constant- the inescapable feeling that death was just one short screech of the brakes away. Thus, I concluded in a very scientific manner that riding in Malaysia must always be akin to the much-acclaimed, children's classic "Mr. Toad's Wild Ride" (or The Wind in The Willows-depending on where you spent your childhood and how far the Disney influence had spread at that time).

Unbeknownst to me, in Malaysia you get to be Mr. Toad's passenger, whether you like it or not, as he rips through life with reckless abandon, cutting off motorists and thinking only of himself. Beep beep, ya bastards!

I never grew accustomed to this experience and thus had taken mental refuge by staring out my side window, where at least I couldn't see what was almost hitting us, well, not most of the time.

In these moments of visual avoidance, I took in some very picturesque hillsides and a few tributes to the urban plight of the city folk. As palm trees, monkeys, and beat up Toyota's zoomed pass my eyes, I could not help but think of how the Malaysian thrill ride is very reminiscent of life in general.

We are all too often rushing past some of the most wonderful things life has to offer, eager to get to our destination. Always focused on tomorrow, avoiding the obstacles in our path by the skin of our teeth, and yet, through all of this, we are missing the beauty of today; the reality of the present and the moments that we will never get back.

Life is a novel that should be enjoyed and read at a leisurely pace whilst you lay out in the sunshine, warming your skin, your heart and your soul... sometimes in the nude. When we are approaching the end of the book we should cling painstakingly to every page, absorbing the fullness of every word, savoring every punctuation mark, and even the occasional spelling error. There is beauty in the commonality of imperfection.

We should never rush to the last page to see how it all turns out, for no matter how amazing and mysterious the closing pages of our life may be, it will all mean nothing if we truly did not enjoy the journey and immerse ourselves in the story.

III
BACK WHEN I THOUGHT I WAS A POET

Falling Apart
10.15.94

All the leaves have fallen now
All the pain is gone
Left behind just twigs and sticks
Branches of what once was

Uncarved Block
08.15.95

A child is born unto the earth
Seeing no boundaries
Knowing not of worth
At peace with life
For now at least
One with nature
Earth and beast

Drowning in a Sea of Root Beer I Find Myself
11.12.95

Fumbling around in the drawer
Searching for things I missed once before

Where nothing is as true to reality as fiction
My own place in the galaxy
Filled with contradiction

How Deep Does a Smile Go?
11.21.95

Where is the line between pleasure and pain
How do we know for sure
Temporary happiness of infinite gloom
Dotted lines so yielding and forgiving
I am those who exist because of their suffering
Destiny
What is it all for
Where can we find the valley in which it lies
Or have the lies which we have been fed covered it
and transformed it into an unrecognizable mass
of green fields and lily white groves
Beneath it is where reality lurks
It breaks through now and then
Only to be interred once again
By the temporary veil of happiness
Welcome to the illusion
We here call it life

View Master
08.05.96

Intelligent beings leading mysterious lives
Drifting through the empty
Viewed through blinded eyes
Non-existent creatures
Governmental lies
Objects full of fantasy
Streak across the skies

Dream Catcher
08.26.96

How much longer must I drive this dark road
before someone shows me the end
Shall I even make it there
Or just stall out around the bend
Take me home

Little Penguin
09.23.96

Would have liked to be a singer
But I wasn't given the voice
Would have liked to be rich
But I wasn't given that choice
There are a lot of things that I would have liked to been
But in reality
I'm just a little penguin

Two Shots of Tequila
05.09.97

Glancing back to childhood through the rearview mirror
Unsettling that in hindsight things are so much clearer
The frame about and empty canvas
My portrait of the future
A blind man's shuffle along a mislaid path
Quite the curious creature
All these things amaze me
Retrospectively getting clearer
But for now I'll just sit right back
And have two shots of tequila

The Day My Father Lost His Hair
09.25.97

There was a certain day in my life
One almost too hard to bear
Gone were the days of childhood bliss
It was now time for a career
I turned to my parents with questions
They looked back at me in despair
For answers seemed to escape them that day
The day my father lost his hair

The Grasshopper
05.21.99

Sometimes it's the little things that seem to pass you by
Most times it's the bigger things with which you're preoccupied
Make time for the little things that made you happy as a child
For it's in those little things
That'll make your life worthwhile

M.H. #9
09.28.99

The glimmer of the sea under the gentle glow of the moon
The twinkle of a shooting star falling from the heavens too soon
Life is fleeting
Like a stolen kiss from the lips of a young gypsy girl
To close your eyes and believe that it all happens for a reason
To trust in what is meant to be

?
10.03.99

I've seen her face in dreams and tasted her lips on the crisp autumn breeze
I've gazed into the stars to see her eyes and watched the sunrise for her smiles

I've touched her skin in the finest silks
I've admired her beauty reflected in the moonlight
I look to the heavens for our destiny

16oz World
02.01.00

Underneath a darkened sky on a stormy summer's eve
The air thick with silence but for the rustling of the leaves
A young man's dreams are crushed and lying broken at his feet
Refracted candle light through an empty beer bottle
Where dreams and reality meet

Wanderlust
02.01.00

To whisper one's worries into a seashell
and cast it into the heart of the they abyss
This is what's meant to truly live
This is what I wish
There's so much of life I've yet to know
Countless places that I wish to go
My mind is filled with curiosity
My heart is adventurous and brave
Setting out riddled with questions
Searching for answers across the waves

An Angel Named Stratus
On the Contemplation of Humanity
02.13.00

Gazing off into the clouds on a not so cloudy day
An angel sits and questions his faith which was lost along the way
Staring down from the heavens
His eyes stormy and full of wonder
Jealousy gathers in his mind and crashes down like thunder
Shadows creep across his soul as a sunny sky turns gray
Feeling so far from where I am on this not so cloudy day

Thoughts of a Modern-Day Viking
or
A Viking Looks at 23
03.03.00

A man looks over the ocean as the wind rustles his hair
The foam on the waves breaks before him as he thinks things he
cannot share
Serenity in solitude
A sojourn for the mind
Searching deep inside himself for things he cannot find
Reflecting back on memories as the water mirrors the sun
To live a life of pleasure and passion
Instead of the things he should have done

Life Is a Twenty-Minute Ride to the Vet
03.09.00

The world rushes by too fast for a dog hanging out the car
window
There's so much to see
There's so much to do
So many things he has no access to
All the plastic people passing by his stare
All the unfamiliar scents floating through the air
The swirling sights and sounds set his furry heart aglow
But the world rushes by too fast for a dog hanging out the car
window

Drinking Beer and Postponing Reality:
An Ode to My Uncle Bub
03.09.00

When it's 2 in the morning and you crawl home to bed
Alone with your thoughts and dreams that are dead
The nights are too lonely
Each minute so long

Fear invading your mind
And you thought you were strong
Waiting for morning
Praying for sunlight
Asking God for the answers
To the questions of the night

Sunset on Galapagos
03.14.00

Little turtle trudging through the tall blades of grass
Studying the simple serenities overlooked as others pass
Tucked away in a fleeting moment
This small being bereft of strife
Tiny steps toward dynamic dreams
Possessing his own quiet confidence in life
It takes so long to achieve so little
But it takes so little to make his day
Wouldn't the world be a much better place
If we all lived life that way

Billy The Kid
03.21.00

Alone on the plains beneath stars so bright
Another lonesome cowboy on another lonesome night
He's traveled by many but remembered by few
A ghost in the wind with a soul black and blue
He cries not for the loss of innocence
But for the betrayal of the heart
Sometimes even legends had dreams that fell apart

The Boy from The Graveyard Speaks
03.27.00

The conversations of the past linger among the leaves of the trees
above
Concrete memorials stand against the winds

Paid for by the ones you love
Secrets held in the eyes of the dead
With no one left to tell
Passing on to another lifetime
Or the lemonade stand on the road to hell
Images set frozen in time
A time that stops for no one
Each stone telling its own story
Under the midday sun

Rocket Pops and Pavlov
03.27.00

For music and bells children flood the streets
With change in their hands but no shoes on their feet
Peering up to the window they shout their requests
Little girls in little dresses
Little boys with bare chests
Popsicles
Snow cones
Ice cream bar treats
The childhood joy of the ice cream man's sweets

Jakob's Laundry
05.02.00

The rusty wheel squeaks as the frayed rope is pulled tight
Shirts
Pants
Unmentionables
All sway in a dark and moonless night
The city street below lying so quiet and so still
An occasional curse or two falls down from the windowsill
The cats below in the garbage peer upward cold with fright
At the silhouette of the woman
In a dark and moonless night

The Revival of Rocky Raccoon
05.02.00

When angels lose their wings and it's clear you've been deceived
Faced with the one who betrayed you
The one whom you once believed
Love is a curious thing
And a curious thing is trust
Both are easily shattered when they are divided by lust
Loving again takes time for the heart is never idle
These were the words that were written inside Gideon's bible

Life On a ¼ Tank
05.17.00

The dead end road to my heart
The painted picture window of my mind
Running on faith and vapors
For I'm out of money and out of time
Will I make it all the way
Only one more exit till home
Or should I just keep on driving
And let my spirit roam

Waiting for Answers
05.18.00

I've had conversations with Orion underneath his stars so bright
Recalling dreams I've never had on a windy summer's night
I asked questions about the future and heard answers about the
past
This is not what I had intended and time was going fast
Why am I here
I shouted to the heavens
But I received no reply
So for now I'll simply remain sitting underneath a purple sky

50% Chance
05.30.00

Lost in a sea of faces
Lost amongst the mighty ocean's roar
One grain in the sands of time
One grain in the sands of the shore
And though she speaks only in whispers
You hear her louder than any other
Swimming against the tide of humanity
Swept adrift
Star-crossed lover

Last Call in My Memory
06.18.00

Sometimes the last lines come before the first
Sometimes the best things start out as the worst
Sometimes clouds just look like clouds
Sometimes angels fall

As a Dog Worries About the Constraints That Time Has Placed
Upon His Life
06.19.00

It's happy hour in Purgatory
It's last call in my mind
Suddenly my world grows stormy
Suddenly my inner thoughts unwind

There are crosses on the roadsides
Reminders here and there
Stirring up strange emotions
Mere transitions to nowhere

Empty faces staring out from magazines
Empty faces that question reality
Slipping through the cracks
In the floorboards of my memory

Lost in Miagi's Garden
07.10.00

Someone told me that the world was melting
Somewhere beyond the Bonsai tree
Behind the chocolate moon apparatus
Someplace that I could not see
And though they tried their best to save it
In the end they'd have to flee
Behind the chocolate moon apparatus
Somewhere beyond the Bonsai tree

Drinking in The Afterlife
09.02.00

There's a bar way down in Bethlehem where a stable used to be
Where salvation comes by the glass
Bought and sold quite easily
A hallowed shelter for lost sheep that stumble in night after night
To drown their shattered dreams underneath the neon lights
A gathering place for wanderers
Resurrecting memories with all their might
Broken hearts with empty bottles
Filling up their lonely nights

Your Shoe – My Hat – Somebody Else's Watch
10.02.00

Sometimes miracles arrive wearing sneakers
Which is not what you'd expect
Singing the unwritten songs of Lennon
Thus commanding much respect

There's no lust like that between enemies
Is what someone once said
And since those words were spoken
I can't get them out of my head

So as I sit here watching traffic
Consulting the horizon for what's right
The world turns into shadows
And the stars come on like streetlights

#7 With Cloudy Eyes
01.15.01

And the sky looked like melting orange creamsicles
Dripping over the cold grey city
However lost to those milling about the charcoal streets below
Like a Picasso to a blind man
The sun sets behind these concrete towers
These 9 to 5 prisons
Built by the inmates themselves
Windows never gazed out of
Trees never climbed
As light yields to the shadows of the corporate landscape

Living on Doane Street
01.29.01

Tomato ripening on the windowsill
Staring defiantly at its future
As the morning sun peeks over the city
Rotting in this landfill of morality
Like everyone else struggling with mortality
Wondering what their legacy will be
The shawl of the specter
Cold with indifference
Washes over those begging prayers of forgiveness on bended knee
We all must ripen

The Ghoul
01.31.01

Sometimes death feels very near
While washing my face
It's right over my shoulder
If I look really close
I can see it in the mirror
Hanging there
Just behind me
Waiting
Waiting
Waiting
I reach for the towel

Fighting Your Ghosts
02.02.01

The bewitching weeds of paranoia wrap around my heart
Choking out my confidence
Strangling my pride
Its roots burrowing deeper
Trying to overtake me
Attempting to separate us
To divide our entwining souls
But my heart burns with passion
Thoughts of you keep me strong
Our lips feeding off of each other's
Nourishing our love

Seashore Lullaby
02.13.01

Impressionable grains of sand squished between my toes
Warm yellow sunrays on my closed eyelids
Producing the most vivid kaleidoscope of colors
Colors like I've never seen
Crisp waves thunder and crack against the shore

Awakening me from my beach blanket crib
I am
Like a child

The Other
02.20.01

The most beautiful of all the angels
With lips as sweet as honey
A tongue as smooth as melted chocolate
Her eyes like black pearls from the deepest darkest ocean
Her hair long and flowing
A waterfall cascading down a physique chiseled and firm
Surrounded by the softest fragrance
A thousand crushed rose petals
Satan is a large breasted woman
Wielding a velvet lined vagina

What the Hell
02.24.01

I've seen the love story in your eyes
I wonder if it's over
It's no longer cuddling
It's fighting for the covers
Your kisses seem distant
Are your thoughts somewhere else
Your eyes are drifting
Leaving me by myself
I don't understand
And you just won't explain
My heart grows weary of playing these games
Talk to me

Yield
03.10.01

Knuckles wrapped around the wheel
Staring down my arm at the open road
Wondering about the future
Lamenting upon the past
Catching the sunset in my rearview mirror
Days like interrupted lines on asphalt rush by my eyes too quickly
The most beautiful things aren't meant to last
And we keep accelerating

Blue Jean Blues
05.12.01

My dreams are faded
Much like my jeans
Comfortable yet torn
Fraying at the seams

Empty are the pockets
Worn is the thread
Ripped apart by reality
In a heap on my bed

So I will stand here naked
And I'll stand here until I'm dead
With my dreams in a heap
On the floor in my head

Overburdened
08.21.01

A lone horse on an abandoned farm
The self-proclaimed King of the Forgotten
Dusty plains and muddy waters caked in the grooves of his hooves
Searching for life's answers among the thistle patch and the briar
bush

Stretching his back
Shaking his head
The dried sand falls from his mane
Shedding each grain like a painful memory
Raising his head toward the horizon
He snorts and stares defiantly at his sunset

U.S. Air 549
10.07.01

Monkey above the clouds
High up in the sky
Goodnight
Goodnight
Sweet banana moon pie

Assorted Nonsense Relevant Only to Now That You May or May
Not Care About
09.19.01

My back hurts when I get out of bed in the morning
I watch my mother become my grandmother a little more each day
The twin towers have been toppled
Bob Dylan has a new album out
I don't buy CDs that the kids are buying anymore
Some people still think Elvis is alive and McCartney is dead
I'd imagine that dying of natural causes is nearly impossible for
ants
I work five days a week for two days off
I do this four weeks a month
Twelve months a year
And I don't know why
We are in the 21st century but where is my rocket pack
Forever the dangling carrot

The Legend of Sauza Jack and Johnny Can-Cun
01.10.02

Two modern day cowboys
Adrift on the streets
Saddled heavy with wisdom
Judging those left behind

Soured by experience
Jaded by lies
Staring down another sunset
Pain burns in their eyes

Having faith in the heavens
Having doubts in humanity
Archangels
Just trying to settle some old scores

The Muse and I
01.10.02

My soul is a clouded marble drifting through the abyss
Searching for the answers amongst the purple fish
My troubled mind trying to comfort my broken heart
My broken heart trying to ease my troubled mind
I'm alone with the sadness of the seventh penguin
Wrestling with angels beneath the peepholes of heaven

Haiku Zero Seven
04.22.02

One finds his smile
Stepping out of the rain clouds
Living for the sun

A Place for Us
04.23.02

I think there is a better place for all of us
Far away from here
Lost between the Northern Lights and the Southern Cross
Somewhere beyond the sun
Somewhere beyond the stars
Beyond the moon
And our dreams

My Mysterious Mistress of Twilight
07.28.02

My dreams are haunted by the song of a woman I've yet to find
Through winding paths sunken in deep lush violet fields
Under the soft golden glow of a laughing moon
I search in vain for a glimpse of her face

The night grows bitterly cold
Chilling the hot blood pumping through me
But yet I wander
Crossing this alternate dreamscape
Longing for her presence
Pining for her touch

Her enchanting melody plays across the emptiness that is this world
Stretching across the void that is my soul

Chlorine Dream
09.10.02

Drowning in emptiness
Waiting for the skies to clear
Love and trust drift away
Damaged beyond repair

So I packed my hope into cardboard boxes

Wrapped my dreams in the faded faces of yesterday's news
Each day rains memories of what we shared
Tomorrow's forecast gives me the blues

For I can only kiss your shadow
Making love to your frail ghost
A tormented angel with clipped wings
Haunted by what he misses most

Through the Window in My Popsicle
12.22.02

And so the little stick man
Took his little stick dog for a walk
Through their little stick world
It was rather uneventful

You and Me and Serendipity
12.22.02

And her navel was warmed by the sun
As she lay outstretched on the grass
Wind playing through her hair
Her laughter carried by the birds back to heaven

Though her eyes were closed she saw for miles
Beyond here and eternity
Spinning slowly in the world of love
Across the universe and back

A ladybug crawled across her toes
And stole her heart away
Forever

The Erotic Misadventures of the Good Cap'n Geech
03.26.03

They say any port in a storm
And it had been raining in old Geech's heart for quite some time
You could hear the rumble of distant thunder in his voice
See the gray clouds gather in his eyes

Beneath his wiry beard sat the stone face of a man
A man who had tasted the bitter salt of reality many a time
Below the stormy appearance laid a heart
A broken heart
Soft as the down of a baby gull

Enter the femme' fatale'

Phenylethylamine
05.25.03

She was a tall girl in a short black dress
Wearing red high heels that clicked like the second hand of a schoolhouse clock
She strolled indifferently across the broken floor tiles of my foolish heart
Following the path of crushed crimson that would lead her straight out of my life
Forever

She was a brunette with the soul of a blonde
I should've known it wasn't going to last
Inevitably I'd be left here in the lonely lounge of my soul
Where it is always last call
And my pockets are filled with nothing but bad karma
Leaving me thirsty for love and for liquor
Wanting
To steal a kiss from the lips of the devil while standing at the gates of heaven

Jamais Vu
06.01.03

In my white room I've had daydreams and nightmares of
sunflakes and snowrays
    Lost between acceptance and denial
    Manipulating the darkness
    Finding comfort in the low hanging moon

    Forever standing at the door to nowhere
    Balancing on the edge of forever
    Peeking through the keyhole to heaven or hell

    Hypnotized by rain drops as they splatter and dance
    Sweet and warm as the forgiveness of God

    When is Jesus due back anyhow

Positively Chad Brown Street
06.15.03

    The rooftops are empty
    All my heroes have gone
    Like doves flying from the roofs of the projects
    My dreams have escaped into the night

    I remain a cloudy pearl in the gutter
    Amongst urine and spilt malt liquor

    Sometimes sadness seems inevitable
    Sometimes the inevitable seems all right

    There's a blue neon cross on the church tower
    Signifying a new neon Christ
    Reinventing the Messiah
    By just a flicker of light

    Somehow heaven appears a little bit closer

In the gutter
In the ghetto
At night

A Mid-Summer Night's Breeze with Just a Hint of Sadness
08.01.03

And so I lay outstretched in a field
Underneath a silver sky
Mercury sliding off of the stars

Piercing my soul
A solitary moonbeam
Letting slip the tears I've held back for so long

Then a quartet of crickets
One playing a banjo
Came to my rescue with their hypnotic melody

Sometimes the Messiah appears as a cricket
Sometimes the Devil shows up in high heels

#5 Revisited
01.06.04

"Just don't fall in love," she said
But by the time those words were spilled over her cherry sweet
lips
It was far too late

For her kisses fell innocently upon me
Virgin snowflakes landing on her blood red stilettos
Melting my soul
Stealing it away

Alone in a darkened room
You'd search the silken desert of her bare shoulders for hours
Convinced that somewhere
There were angel's wings

Yet in a flash you'd find the devil in her eyes
A dancing flame of desire locked behind mascara

The most desired of the desirable
Lying just a heartbeat away
"I'm sleepy," she whispers
"Tell me a story"
And suddenly
Like a child
I am lost

My Life in Magnetic Poetry
08.11.04

I sit and wait for my angel to appear
Her wings dipped in moonlight
Feathery soft salvation
A shield of plumage against the harsh inequities on the world

My patchwork princess
Lips tasting of forbidden green apples
Eyes wide and haunting
My perversion of paradise

A red devil dreaming of a goddess in white lace
Sitting in a dark room waiting for my life to develop
We are just a dream away from yesterday
Tomorrow is closing in fast

Searching for Purple Fish
02.10.05

Sometimes you have to believe in who you are
Even when you're not too sure
Bet against the odds
A thousand to one across the board

Orion weeps for all of us
Though sometimes there's no reason to cry

Climbing up an icicle
Arm wrestling the wind
Who says it can't be done

Searching for strawberry colored rays of sunshine
Within a murky emotional abyss
Forever damned by the ticking of the clock
Surrounded by hypocrisy in the pumpkin patch

I'm king of my own sandcastle
Prove me wrong

All for Beans
05.23.07

He was almost 30
He was doing all right
Though he worked all day
And he worked all night

"I do it all for Beans" is what he'd say
She was his tiny daughter
His sweet bay-bay

Caroline
10.01.16

Careful not to be deceived.
The others spin a web of lies.
Be wary when you get all that you wish.
Don't let them sew buttons on your eyes.

Eternal Fall
10.15.16

I want to live in eternal fall;
The roads lined with crunchy orange, red, and brown leaves that swirl, twist and dance, whilst I walk alone.

My Phantom Love
10.31.16

In my mind I'm ballroom dancing with the ghost of a girl I've never seen,
Yet somehow I've always known.
Our spirits… forever entwined.

Serendipity
12.11.16

She guarded her heart fiercely.
Kept it chained away and safe.
Somehow he held the key to every lock.

Her smile could've stolen the stars from the sky,
if the twinkle in her eyes hadn't already done so.

Her words are poetry, like candy to my soul.
She creates and satiates my hunger at the same time.
Pleasing me and leaving me wanting… more.

Kismet
1.19.17

She had a tune in her heart and bells on her toes.
Her essence, a beautiful melody; her soul, a sweet song.

IV
CURRENTLY ME

Unleash Your Inner Rock Star

So here you are. Every previous year, every day, every hour, every moment and minuscule decision, right or wrong, has led to this. So now what?

Do you crumble under the pressure?

Do you fall apart?

Do you make a half-hearted effort so that when you fail, you can say that you didn't give it your all?

Or do you unleash your inner rock star, and completely make the situation your own?

When people hear the word "rock star" there is a variety of names and images that may come to mind based on one's musical preference and time. The one thing they will all have in common is that the image will be of someone whom commands a room, who has a presence that can light up a stage and bring thousands of people to their feet. That can be you- and should be you.

Back in college, I did a presentation for public speaking called "The Art of Self-Projection". It was based on the idea that no one is going to believe in you if you do not believe in yourself. Great leaders, charismatic speakers, the people that others look up to are those who aren't afraid to show who they are. Those that can convey in a positive way what they believe in and what they represent. These people exude that intangible element that makes others just feel good about themselves and the situation at hand.

Simply harnessing this intangible and making it a reality for yourself can change your life, regardless of past mistakes.

Timothy Mouse, the little vermin that befriended Dumbo in the Disney classic animation of the same name, gave the pint-sized pachyderm an ordinary feather and told him it was magical—and as long as Dumbo held onto it tightly, he could fly. The truth of course was that Dumbo could fly all along and Timothy knew this or he wouldn't have cast his lot in with him, but he just needed to find a way to get Dumbo to believe it, to get Dumbo to unleash his inner rock star and soar to new heights.

Some of us still think we need that magic feather, and unfortunately there are many whose feather has taken them down the wrong path, as countless individuals have turned to drugs and alcohol for the confidence they think they need, only to end up in ruin; ruin that need not be permanent, if only they know how to pull out of that tailspin and return to greatness.

So how do you walk into a room and get noticed by everyone in it? How do you close the big deals and lead the big wheels? How do you use what you've been given to inspire others to do the same? It must come from within. You must know who you are and where your faith lies.

Faith is the great immeasurable element that fuels our soul. Faith powers that inner being much, much more than having ridiculously awesome hair, 80s sunglasses and ripped up jeans could ever dream to do. That's my image of a rock star. I am a child of the 1980s.

I personally have been comforted in many dark situations by the grace of God, the power of the Holy Spirit, and the love of Christ. My confidence, serenity, and overwhelming feeling of control over the situations that present themselves before me are all deeply rooted within my soul, nourished by the word of God and watered daily by prayer.

This is your moment. There will not be any other exactly like it. What is fueling the rock star inside you? How much longer till you decide to tap into all that is good and is of love? Only you have those answers. Only you can make the change that you want in your life and in this world. We are His body, we are His blood—we have the power to do what is right.

Rock on and God bless.

It was the last day of school for Beans, my daughter, on Tuesday the 21st of June 2016. I wanted to do something special for her, as she was just finishing up the third grade. Time seems to be going quicker these days, quicker for me than I would like it to be; the non-stop hustle and bustle of it all. Each day seemingly filled more and more with the plastic nonsense of this world rather than the things of substance; soulful, loftier things. I can clearly recall the day of her birth 9 years ago, when the doctor handed her over to the nurse to be cleaned and little Beans grabbed me by my pinky finger; nothing has ever been the same since.

So, to make the most of the opportunity in front of me, I hurried home from work and made it there in time to pick her up and whisk her off to the movies despite the traffic that attempted to thwart our path. We went to see *Alice Through the Looking Glass*, the follow up to *Alice In Wonderland*. The theater was empty when we went in and so we could take our usual seats in the middle of the top row. With a large tub of buttered popcorn between us, and a swirled slushy in our hands, we embarked on a fantastic journey of whimsy along with Dorothy, Hatter, and their friends. My daughter has a slight cat obsession, so Cheshire is her clear favorite. The movie was quite enjoyable and I was thankful for our time together. Interesting thought in retrospect as so much of the movie was about time itself.

As I try to do quite often, I make efforts to add to our experiences with a little next level idea. This time I had purchased some Alice characters for one of our video game systems and had them nestled in the passenger seat of Maggie May, my big blue Dodge Ram truck, for my daughter to find upon our return. She was quite excited to see them and climbed up into the cab. As I went around the other side and slid behind the wheel, Beans drew my attention to a solitary red plastic shopping cart that sat alone in the parking lot beneath a streetlight.

There were no immediate stores near the movie theater so she wanted to know where it was from. I explained that there were quite a bit of stores in the shopping plaza as it was about a half of a mile in length. That answer did not quite satisfy her curiosity, so moments later there we were, the two of us joining the lonely red carriage under the buzzing glow of the flickering streetlight.

The little red carriage had the name of a liquor store upon its side in tiny white print. She asked me where that store was and I explained it was at the other end of the plaza, the very last store. She didn't even need to ask the next question, for in my heart I knew this night would see the two of us escorting the wayward cart back to its rightful place in the world.

"But Daddy, it's an outcast! It's a misfit! We have to bring it back! Can we?" she exclaimed as she grabbed the shiny metal handlebar and looked up to me for approval. I agreed and saddled up alongside her to start our little quest through the empty parking lot.

As we walked through the plaza past the gymnasium, the breakfast diner, and the materials store, we had a great little discussion about misfits and outcasts and how we should always look out for each other. She named the cart "Rickety" as it did have a penchant for wobbling along the asphalt. But, as rickety as he was, he still should be with his family, and we were just the people to bring him there according to my little one.

I explained to her, as best a father of 39 can to his daughter of 9 years, that we are all called to help each other through this life. Kindness is what matters. Having a helpful heart, despite the circumstances and the opinions of those around us, we must do what we know to be right. It is a big lesson; a lesson that some people sadly never seem to learn, yet one that is so very key to our human experience. Perhaps some might think it is too big a lesson for a small child and a red shopping cart named Rickety, but I feel it is a lesson that knows no age limit. Plus, who knows when I might have time to teach it again?

As we strolled up to the closed liquor store behind the red plastic frame and the shimmering handlebar of the once lost shopping cart, we corralled two more strays that went unnamed, and returned them all to the front of the store, parking them beneath the still glowing neon signs. The other carts all sat inside the glass windows staring at us.

My daughter pushed on the handle of the cart once more, saying, "There you go. You're home now."

Tim Burton's work with Lewis Carroll's *Alice Through the Looking Glass* was very well done, but the story of Rickety is the one I will always remember fondly.

A Lost Boy Turns 39
07.12.16

I was born 39 years ago today, July 12, 1977. Since then I have traveled the world. My feet have walked upon 6 continents, 23 countries, and more states here in the U.S.A. than I can remember.

I have seen the mighty coliseum of Rome. I traveled to Paris and walked beneath the graceful beauty of the Eiffel Tower. I walked the streets of Prague and the outback of Australia. The plains of Africa, the cobblestone streets of jolly old England, the beaches of Rio, I have wandered through all of these and more in search of answers that never seem to appear.

Despite being socially acceptable by the plastic standards of the shallow end of society, I have never quite felt at home. I get comfortable. I adjust. There are places I'd rather be, but I never have felt that I truly fit in with this world. This reality has never seemed to be real to me, as it does to most others. I never feel free here. Perhaps like the Lost Boys from the Peter Pan story of old, I am in search of Neverland.

My innocence has always been something I have closely guarded. In many ways, I refuse to grow up and conform to that which is considered to be an adult mindset. The corporate world and the concrete jungle that the convicts have constructed for themselves whilst strutting about in their suits and ties, it never has appealed to me, none of it. Not for an instant. It was as far from reality as I want to be. The tie is a noose. It would never allow me to be free.

"The death of Santa Claus is your own." I penned those words so many moons ago when I was in back in high school. I stand by them today as complete truth. For I feel that there are certain turning points in our lives that change us forever, but only if we let them. Reality is what we deem it to be. Me? I choose to believe.

I have a Christmas heart. I keep a merry old soul full of joy, caring, generosity, and love for all mankind all year round. My Christmas spirit does not get boxed up with the rest of the ornaments on December 26th, nor does it get thrown out into the street like a dried-up Christmas tree; discarded like a prom dress, cherished and then abandoned.

I may forever feel like a square boy in a round world, but that is okay. It merely means that this world cannot contain me with its make-believe parameters. Who is to say that the reality in my head is not what is truly real? I define what I will accept as acceptable. Dreams versus reality – the choice is yours.

I am a dreamer. I am a believer. I know that things in this world are not what they seem to be. For we are spiritual beings going through a human experience on this earth, our island home. None of this is real in the real sense of the word.

A lyric to a currently popular song by artist Ruth B states that, "Neverland is home to Lost Boys like me, and Lost Boys like me are free." I couldn't agree more, as this Lost Boy starts his 39th year, far away from reality, which is where I want to be.

And as one of my country music heroes David Allan Coe once sang, "You like to live in the city. I like to live in my head."

No matter where I may be, I will tell you this, I am always happy, which is more than I can say for most.

Going Forward You Should Just Keep Going Forward

At a point in your life where you simply don't know where to go? Go forward.

The future can be scary. It may be hard to continue on one's path. People often get frozen in their tracks and simply take refuge upon the couch in front of the television. Sadness sometimes creeps in and never moves on. It lingers. It sits on the couch with you and hogs the remote. It orders pizza but does not chip in.

We sometimes fall into a quagmire of our past that is so vast it encroaches upon every aspect of our lives, preventing us from going on, from going forward. We become slaves to our yesterdays. Chained up by our memories. Believing we are incapable of doing better, of moving on. We read the labels placed upon us by others and we start to believe them. We tattoo them upon our hearts. They become our identity.

It has been my experience that in times of trouble it is best not to linger, and to simply keep moving forward. Focus upon your next step and take it wisely. Don't set your sights so far down the road that you render yourself incapable of just making a small advance each day. Rip off those labels placed upon you by others. Crush them underfoot, shake them from your sandals, and move forward.

We all have struggles. We all have pain. We all end up scarred. That commonality is not a hallmark sign of defeat. It is merely evidence of a life well lived, and it is a beautiful thing. Take comfort in that. You are not alone. We are never alone.

Just keep going forward for life is a game of inches. A small daily victory is still a victory, and victories add up over time. As you travel, as you journey, you will fall, you will get hurt, you will struggle, you will grow, and you will go forward.

In time, you may glance back and see that old version of yourself sitting way back in the past, eating pizza on the couch next to sadness, and you may barely recognize the person that you once were. It is okay to glance back, but do not linger, go forward.

Go forward in faith, not in fear. Shadows are only proof that there is light. Darkness can never conquer you and squelch out your light unless you let it. When you see the shadows creeping in and find yourself being enveloped by darkness, keep your eyes on the horizon and simply go forward, letting that light inside you power you onward, taking that next step.

This game isn't over unless you give up. There is always a way. There is always a path. It may not be easy. It will not be easy. But if you want it, trust me, it's worth it. Just keep going forward.

A Thing For Misfits

For fifteen years now, I have worked for the same company, which specializes in facial, oral, and cosmetic surgery. In the past 3 years I have been working under the label of COO, Chief Operations Officer, of the company. I manage two offices, in two states, currently with two doctors and eighteen employees. In the previous years there, I worked in surgery as an anesthesia assistant. I still assist in surgery from time to time, as I like to stay busy, stay involved, and stay helpful. It has been an interesting and rewarding career that has allowed me to grow within the company, and for that I am thankful.

Part of my responsibilities as COO is to manage the office, which includes hiring new employees. The interview process is an interesting one. Resumes are all the same, some slightly better constructed than others, but all basically they are all like a pig wearing lipstick. There is truth in there, but you have to dig past the aesthetic portion of it to find it.

A receptionist who worked with us for years told me that she noticed that I have a thing for misfits. Some of the employees I hire may not be the most qualified personnel for the job, but they seem to be the most deserving of a break in life. Patients that are in a bit of a bind and struggling financially, I go out of my way to structure payment plans for, and I work with them to ensure they will receive the care that they need. I'm the type of guy that sees the beauty in imperfection. I recognize the shared human struggle.

In all aspects of life I look out for the little guy. I cheer for the underdog. I bet heavy on the long shots. I align myself with others that may not be the biggest in the fight, but that have the biggest heart.

I often think of myself as King Moonracer from the old Rudolph The Red-Nosed Reindeer Christmas special by Rankin & Bass. The King was a flying lion that soared high above the Island of Misfit Toys. He kept an eye on each of them, and even lingered behind when the misfits went off to homes, so that other misfits who wandered would not find themselves alone there.

I believe in the dreams of the dreamers. I believe in love. I believe in magic. I believe we all need a little help from time to time. And I believe, that if you never give up, it will always work out all right. Maybe it will not be how you thought it would turn out, but it may even turn out better.

So if, whilst traveling throughout this life, you find yourself a little down, lost, and out of town. Rest well knowing that everything will work out, and until it does, I'll be here flying high above, keeping an eye out for you. After all, I have a thing for misfits.

ABOUT THE AUTHOR

Dustin makes his home with his wife and daughter in scenic New England. He works in healthcare and has also done his share of paranormal reality television. His true passion is helping others and giving motivational lectures. He is admittedly a bit wonky and quite proud of it. Dustin enjoys spending time in remote places that only God knows exists. He loves warm Italian bread, pizza, pumpkin pie, and Double Stuf Oreos.

Dustin J. Pari

Made in the USA
Middletown, DE
24 June 2021

42255012R00118